WOOD AND WOODWORKING TOOLS

Wood and Woodworking Tools

A Handbook

E.G. RICHARDS, ROBERT PLUMPTRE,
and STUART WILSON

Edited by Laila Monahan

INTERMEDIATE TECHNOLOGY PUBLICATIONS
on behalf of THE REFUGEE STUDIES PROGRAMME,
OXFORD UNIVERSITY 1989

Intermediate Technology Publications Ltd
103/105 Southampton Row, London WC1B 4HH, UK

Refugee Studies Programme
University of Oxford
Queen Elizabeth House
International Development Centre
21 St. Giles, Oxford, OX1 3LA

ISBN 185339 025 9

Typeset by J&L Composition, Ltd, Filey, North Yorkshire
Printed in Great Britain by Short Run Press, Exeter

Contents

The authors would like to thank the Nuffield Foundation for the generous grant which made this project possible.

They would also like to thank the Refugee Studies Programme, Queen Elizabeth House, Oxford University which co-ordinated the project and provided editorial support from its inception.

The authors also wish to acknowledge the importance of the contribution made by the three artists who have illustrated this book—Miss Lorna Impey, Mr Peter Reddy and Mrs Victoria Caulcut.

Introduction

Men have worked wood with metal tools for several thousand years and there is still a remarkable similarity between some of the earliest carpenters' tools and those in use today. Of course, in industrial countries, woodworking is now largely mechanized, and even the amateur handyman will often prefer portable power tools to traditional hand tools.

Frequently, when giving advice and aid to Third World countries, professionals in the field of woodworking focus their attention—and rightly so—on the mechanization of rural craft industries. But in many situations it is still appropriate to use hand tools, particularly in Third World countries where abundant labour will serve in some measure to offset the problems of limited resources, funds or unreliable sources of energy for mechanization. In countries where it is difficult to get the foreign exchange to buy spare parts to maintain sawmills, a pitsaw can still be a practical means of producing planks from a log.

Thus, this handbook describes a range of hand tools and simple muscle-powered machinery. It is notable that, over the years, specific progress in the development of manually operated tools has been made by merely responding to the knowledge that power generated by the leg is stronger than that of the hand. Indeed many of the most effective 'hand tools' are at least in part 'leg tools'. To complement the list of basic tools, a brief description has been included of the elements of sawmilling and of low-cost powered saws for converting round logs into sawn wood.

Those carpenter's tools essential for the production of simple furniture and other everyday items are detailed together with some other tools which are desirable if not essential. The list owes much to the work of 'Tools for Self-Reliance' (TFSR), an organization which meets the practical needs of the Third World by collecting, refurbishing and despatching tools to needy organizations and groups of carpenters.

It must be stressed that this handbook is not aimed at Third World carpenters and other craftsmen themselves. They will be

[1]

familiar with much of the subject matter already. Rather it is written for those organizations and individuals in the industrialized countries which are in a position to give aid to developing countries either in cash or in kind.

This illustrated catalogue of basic tools and equipment should help facilitate communication between aid agency staff and local carpenters by enabling craftsmen to show aid workers exactly which tools they need for their specific purposes. The value of this should not be underestimated for it is all too easy to look for blanket solutions when providing aid, forgetting that specific requirements and the complexity of tools and skills will vary considerably in different areas. So, keeping in mind the basic tenets of intermediate technology—that you must build on the existing skills, resources, and equipment available in a given area—much waste and duplication can be avoided and incalculable goodwill and trust established between the field workers and those they hope to help. The student of carpentry too would do well to remember this approach when setting out to 'improve' on the work of his predecessors.

This handbook can also serve a valuable secondary purpose. The brief period of semi-industrialization which many countries experienced over the last half-century, along with the import of mass-produced goods from industrialized countries, has helped to kill off village crafts such as wood turning. In some cases, local knowledge of the techniques involved in these crafts has been lost. So the chapter on simple lathes and other equipment could help revive the use of the simple devices that were in regular use even in industrial countries until a few decades ago, and could certainly have a useful role in areas where labour is plentiful but electric power is not.

As a compendium of simple tools and basic methods, this handbook also has a definite value as an introductory textbook for those teaching woodwork at both theoretical and practical levels in developing countries, and to refugees who have had the continuity of both traditional skills and familiar materials disrupted. Whether in schools or in camps, this book will itself prove a useful tool.

In some areas sawmills will provide the carpenter with a range of sawn wood as well as a probable supply of off-cuts—so-called waste wood—that can also serve as perfectly good raw material for the wood turner and the carpenter. But in other areas wood

[2]

may be available only in the round; so a further section of the book summarizes the steps needed to convert a tree into planks and to season (dry) them sufficiently for their intended use. Because it is simple to make, very effective, and cheap to run, a solar drying kiln is described.

Finally, although to many the importance of trees themselves seems so self-evident as not to merit consideration, a brief explanation of the growth cycle of trees and their vital place in the ecology of all living things is included. Unless active consideration is given to their careful husbandry and replacement even while we are trying to alleviate the various and numerous problems of the Third World using whatever resources are available, not only will this brief handbook be useless but the lives of the people we are trying to help will certainly be lost.

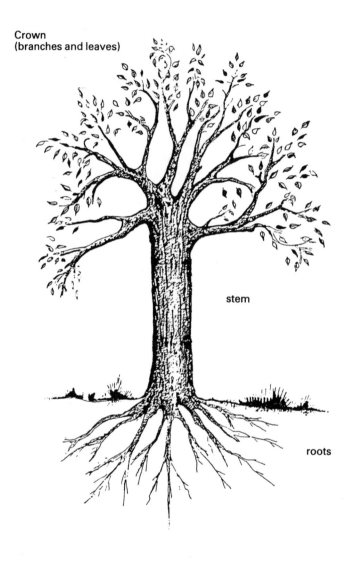

Crown
(branches and leaves)

stem

roots

Fig. 1.1
Diagram of tree showing crown stem and branches.

[4]

CHAPTER ONE
Trees and their uses

Trees are found almost everywhere except in deserts and on the tops of high mountains. They are essential to our existence and to the environment in which we live. Besides producing useful products they are vital in many other ways, and before they are cut down it is necessary to know their value and to consider whether their value standing is greater than their value felled. It is senseless to cut them down if the environment in which we live is spoiled as a result. It is certainly worth reminding ourselves of the particular value of trees. Trees:

○ protect land, people, animals and plants from too much wind, sun, and rain;

○ take water and useful minerals from deep in the soil, bring the minerals to the soil surface for use by other plants and animals and release the water into the atmosphere to make it more humid and less drying;

○ slow down the rate of movement of air and its drying effects on soil and surrounding agricultural crops;

○ cool the air by evaporation of water from their leaves. They shade the soil and prevent it getting as hot and dry, and as cold, as it would without them. Forests are cool when it is hot and warm when it is cold;

○ hold the soil with their roots thus preventing its being blown away by the wind or washed away by heavy rain;

○ provide humus from dead leaves which collect underneath the trees, which holds water like a sponge thus stopping it from running too fast through the soil and off its surface. The humus provides food for small animals such as worms and termites that make holes in the soil, which in turn allow water to penetrate into rather than run off its surface;

○ in large forests, are thought to influence the climate. It is difficult to prove the exact influence large forests have, but it is probably considerable; they do reduce the danger of soil erosion and desertification.

○ provide fruits and leaves many of which can be eaten by man or animals, particularly domestic animals;

○ provide fuel wood for heating and cooking;
○ provide wood for making many things—the specific subject of this book

Trees take a long time to grow and should be cut down only if others are planted to replace them. If this is not done, the result may be flooding, soil erosion or the creation of deserts.

Parts of the tree

It is necessary to know how a tree works before one can really understand how to use its wood. Trees have three main parts: the roots, the stem (or trunk, or bole) and the crown (see Fig. 1.1).

The roots grow down into the soil, hold the tree firm and suck up minerals and water which are passed up the stem and used to make new wood, bark, leaves and roots.

The stem holds the crown up where it can get light and air. It

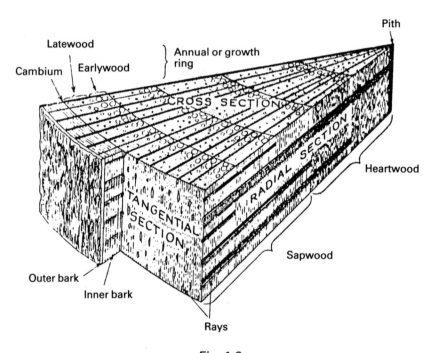

Fig. 1.2

Section of tree showing the main wood characters (BRE Princes Risborough.)

[6]

also passes water and minerals upwards from the roots, and food materials downwards.

The crown consists of branches which spread the leaves out to catch energy from sunlight, carbon dioxide gas from the air, and water and minerals to make food materials. These are then carried around to the parts of the tree where there are growing cells, and there they are made into new wood, bark, roots or leaves. The whole of the tree, except for the fully grown leaves, is covered with a layer of these growing cells called the 'cambium'.

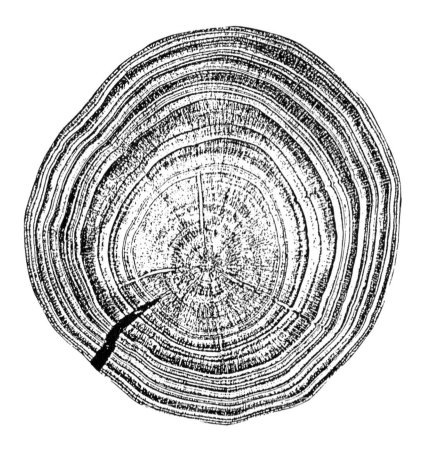

Fig. 1.3
Photograph of the cross section of a tropical conifer tree showing the pattern of rings. (OFI Oxford.)

[7]

The cambium on the trunk and branches of the tree produces wood cells on the inside and bark cells on the outside.

Fig. 1.2 shows a piece cut out of a stem or branch of a tree. Fig. 1.3 is a photograph of a finely sanded disc cut from a conifer grown in the tropics showing growth rings which are comprised of bands of thin-walled cells alternating with bands of thicker-walled cells.

The whole tree is made up of millions of small cells most of which are too small to be seen without a microscope. Figs. 1.4, 1.5, and 1.6 show cells, magnified by a microscope, of a

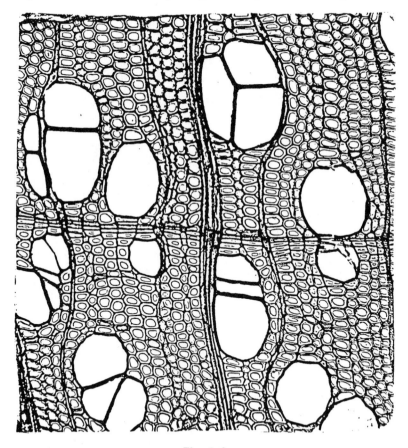

Fig. 1.4
Microscopic view of section of hardwood cut transversely (across the grain) (OFI Oxford).

[8]

hardwood timber cut across the stem (Fig. 1.4), along the stem radially to the stem (Fig. 1.5), and along the stem tangentially to (Fig. 1.6). (See also Fig. 1.2 which shows the cutting planes in a section of the stem.) The figures show large cells, called 'vessels', which transport water and other substances up the stem. The smaller cells running up and down the stem are 'fibres', the main function of which is to give strength to the stem, and the bundles of cells running from the centre of the tree to the outside are

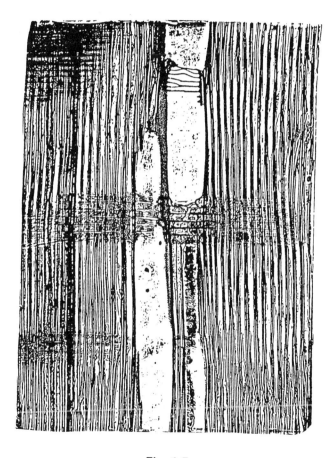

Fig. 1.5
Microscopic view of hardwood cut along the grain to show the radial surface of the wood (from the centre of the tree to the outside) (OFI Oxford).

[9]

'rays', the function of which is the storage and transport of water and food materials radially in the stem. Conifer trees do not have vessels but instead have 'tracheids'; otherwise they are not very different from the broadleaved tree shown here.

Earlywood, latewood and tree rings

As the tree grows the cambium produces new cells; the inside cells turn into wood cells. Early in the growing season, when

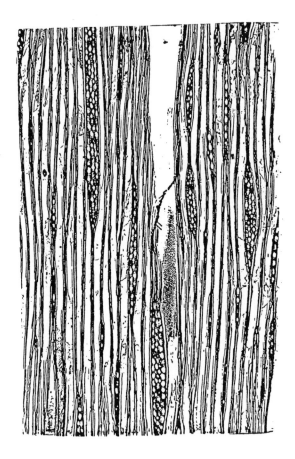

Fig. 1.6
Microscopic view of hardwood cut along the grain at a tangent to the tree stem (at right angles to the radius) (OFI Oxford).

[10]

growth is rapid and there is plenty of water, large cells with thin walls are grown. Later in the season growth slows down, less water needs to be transported and smaller cells with thicker walls are grown which give heavier, stronger wood. The first is known as 'earlywood' and the second 'latewood'.

Dry weather or, in temperate climates, cold weather tends to stop growth altogether. When growth starts again there is a sharp change from latewood to earlywood. This produces a 'growth ring'; each growth ring has both earlywood and latewood in it.

If there is just one dry season or winter each year only one ring is produced per year, but if, as in some of the wetter tropical countries, there are several wet and dry seasons in a year, more than one ring may be produced and it will not then be possible to tell the age of a tree from the number of rings in it.

Sapwood and heartwood

The outer wood beneath the cambium is used to conduct water and minerals up the tree while the inner bark outside the cambium is used to bring food materials down from the leaves. As the tree grows, wood is left further and further inside the tree and stops conducting water. At this stage it often becomes filled with gums, resins or tannins which may be waste products from the tree but which protect the wood by preventing rotting by fungus or attack by insects. This inner wood is called 'heartwood' while the actively conducting wood is called 'sapwood'. Sapwood usually contains starch which is food for both insects and fungi and is, therefore, usually less durable and more liable to attack than heartwood.

Sapwood, however, being conductive, can be penetrated by solutions of preservatives which make it resistant to rot and insect attack.

Shrinkage

Wood swells when wet and shrinks when dry but, because of the arrangement of the cell walls and substances within them, it shrinks most around the circumference of the rings (tangentially), less from the centre of the tree outwards (radially) and very little along the length of the tree or branch (longitudinally). This variation in shrinkage leads to problems of cracking, bending and twisting when drying wood and making furniture.

Timber which includes the centre of the tree (the pith or heart) almost always distorts and cracks as it dries because the tangential shrinkage is greater than the radial. Care, therefore, should be taken to avoid having pith in timber when stability is required.

Seasoning

Timber being made into furniture must be dried to the moisture content it will reach when left for a long time in the place where it is to be used. Otherwise the furniture will crack or twist in some way. Sometimes this can be done by air-drying in stacks or open-sided sheds, but in most climates this does not dry the wood to the moisture content needed and the timber has either to spend a long time in a closed building, or it has to be dried in a special heated chamber (a seasoning kiln) which will dry it relatively quickly.

Wood density

The wood density, or weight of a given volume of water such as a cubic foot or cubic centimetre, depends on the quantity of cell wall compared with the quantity of 'hole' (lumen) in the cells of the wood. As all wall substance is similar for all trees, it is quantity which largely determines density. Ebony, for instance, contains 75–80% cell wall while balsa wood has only 10–20%. The density affects the strength and hardness of the wood and also the ease with which it is cut and worked by hand or machine.

Grain

The size and arrangement of the cells give the 'grain' of wood, and the contents of the cells and cell walls determine its colour. Open or coarse-grained woods have large cells while close or fine-grained woods have smaller ones. Woods are normally considered decorative because they have attractive colours and grain patterns. Interlocked grain, found mainly in tropical woods, occurs when the grain spirals around the tree, first in one direction and at a later period in the opposite direction. Wavy grain occurs when cells grow in uneven waves up and around the stem.

Methods of using wood

Trees can be used in the round, without shaping, apart from cross cutting them to the right length, as poles or posts or even in furniture as round legs, but normally wood is cut and shaped to give the desired form.

Cleaving

Shaping can be accomplished by cleaving or splitting the wood. Only trees with a fairly straight grain are suitable for splitting. As trees with interlocked grain are not suitable, only a fairly small number of woods are good for cleaving. 'Cleavage strength' is a property which is measured by finding the force needed to split a standard-sized sample of that species; it gives a good measure of the ease of splitting a particular wood.

Sawing

Sawing uses sharp metal teeth to cut wood. The tooth design is different for cutting across the grain (cross-cutting teeth) than for cutting along the grain (ripping teeth). For the first an upright tooth is used to slice across the cells while for the second a forward pointing tooth is used to chisel through the fibres. Saws can operate as reciprocating saws allowing a forward and backward motion of the blade. All hand-operated saws and some mechanical saws are of this type. Circular saws are round metal plates with teeth cut around their edges which rotate around a central spindle. Bandsaws are simply a band of metal with teeth cut into the edges, running around two wheels. Circular and band saws are almost always powered by motors of one kind or other.

Sawing of timber from logs is normally done when they are still wet (unseasoned) and the wood is sawn into different widths and thicknesses according to what sizes are required. The sawn wood then needs to be dried (seasoned) before it is made into any other product. Saws for cutting wet wood need to have different tooth shapes from saws for cutting dry wood because the wood is more fibrous and 'woolly' when wet and harder and more brittle when dry. It is impossible to get a good smooth finish on wood if it is sawn wet, or with a blunt saw.

Turning

Turning is carried out by rotating a piece of wood on a 'lathe' and bringing up a stationary tool against the wood to shape it (see page 78).

[13]

Planing

Planing is used to smooth the surface of dry wood. In planing, cutting normally follows along the grain rather than across it as in turning. The wood must be dry and the tools sharp to get good, smooth results.

Boring

Most woods can be bored given reasonable care, and with support around and underneath the timber being bored.

Nailing

The ease with which nails can be driven into wood, the power with which they are retained, and the tendency to split are important considerations. The harder and heavier a wood, the more difficult it is to drive nails into it. At densities over 0.80 grams/cubic centimeter (50 pounds/cubic foot) at 12% wood moisture content, it becomes very difficult to knock nails into dry wood without bending them, and pre-boring of holes is necessary. The denser and harder a wood is the greater is the tendency to split when nailed, and woods with low cleavage strengths are worse than the more resilient species. Woods that cleave well therefore normally nail rather badly. Low density woods very seldom split badly. Low density woods, or woods with low-density early wood, tend to hold nails badly while woods that split when nailed also have low retention strength. It is easier to nail green (wet) timber than dry timber, and nails tend to split it less.

Screws

Pre-boring is necessary for screws except in the lowest density woods, and most woods can be screwed successfully if properly bored first. Again low-density woods and woods with wide bands of low-density early wood retain screws particularly badly where the screw does not go through bands of latewood. Fast growing woods with wide rings and a high contrast in density between early and latewood are bad for screwing, therefore. Also, it must be noted that screws are not normally used along the grain since they will not hold well.

Dowelling

Wooden pegs (dowels) driven into pre-bored holes form a very effective joint because they are usually thicker than screws or

[14]

nails and are less likely to move sideways in the wood when a joint is stressed.

Gluing

Most woods can be glued if dry, but gluing is sometimes ineffective with oily or waxy woods with very high density which do not absorb water easily. Some types of glue are made from natural products such as animal or fish bones, but most are made from synthetic resins as these are, unlike the animal glues, water-resistant.

Smoothing and finishing

When making furniture and other articles where the value will be increased by good appearance, it is important to smooth and finish the wood surface with wax, oil, paint or varnish. Oils of various kinds, usually locally available, can be cheap and may be suitable for wood finishing if conventional finishes are not available or are too expensive. Similarly, pumice stones or other fine abrasives can form substitutes for sandpaper. Finishes not only improve appearance but can also prevent attack by wood boring insects or rot.

Most woods can be finished if enough effort is expended but the very soft woolly woods, and those with coarse, open grains, are the most difficult. Interlocked grains will also often give finishing problems. Hard dense woods require more energy to finish but give a good hard-wearing surface, and retain their appearance longer, than softer woods. Good oil finishes often preserve wood better, require less maintenance and last longer than paints or varnishes, particularly when exposed to sunlight.

Most woods will tend to darken with exposure to light and, to some extent, lose their attractive appearance. Exposed to the elements they weather to a uniform silvery-grey colour but good finishes can prevent this happening.

It is important, therefore, to know the species of wood available for use, their characteristics and how to dry, cut, shape, joint, smooth and finish them to get the best results. It is all-important that sufficient care is taken at each stage of the process to ensure a good result. This does not necessarily mean doing more work; it merely requires that the right operation be carried out at the right time.

[15]

Finally, if it is not essential to cut a tree down, do not do it! The tree is probably useful where it is. Economy in use of wood is very important in many parts of the world. It normally takes over fifty years for a tree to grow large enough to produce wood suitable for making furniture. An essential part of good husbandry is to consider the generations to come who will need trees to survive.

CHAPTER TWO

Production and care of sawnwood—saws and sawmills

Round logs have been cut into square-edged timber for thousands of years. Axes or adzes have been used to square-off logs (see Chapter 3) to make large beams or posts. Although this method is still used in places, it is wasteful and thus the normal method now is to saw with a thin band of metal with notches cut out of it so that the remaining sharp points or 'teeth' cut the fibres of the wood. Teeth of varying shapes are designed specifically to cut in different directions and for hard or soft woods. The process of preparing and maintaining saws of different kinds is called 'sawdoctoring.'

Types of saw
Almost all hand operated saws are of the 'push-pull' (reciprocating) type. Saws cutting across the log or the grain of the wood are 'cross-cut' saws while saws cutting along the grain of the wood, as is done when cutting planks from a log, are called 'rip' saws. Cross-cut saw teeth are fairly upright, designed to slice across the grain using the sharp point of the tooth, while rip saws are designed to chisel away the fibres and are forward pointing or 'hooked'. The angle of 'hook' depends on the timber to be cut, the saw type and the power used to drive the saw.

The reciprocating type of saw, used at least 3000–4000 years ago, was in mediaeval times in Europe developed into a sawmill powered by water or wind, or manually by methods such as cranking handles operated by two or more people. In the eighteenth century the circular saw, a circular metal plate with teeth around its circumference, was developed and patented. In 1808, a bandsaw—an endless steel band with teeth on one side, rotating around two wheels—was developed and patented (Fig. 2.1 (a)).

Methods of powering sawmills other than by hand or animal power led to these developments and subsequently to conventional modern sawmills. Sawmills are now extremely costly, however, and most require that logs are brought to them, thereby

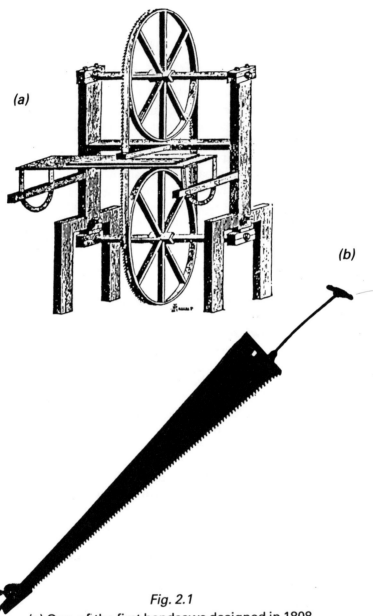

Fig. 2.1
(a) One of the first bandsaws designed in 1808.
(b) A Pitsaw.

involving the use of heavy machinery to transport the logs from the forest to the mill. In remote areas where the available quantity of logs is small, it is uneconomic to use conventional sawmills and alternative methods or apparatus have to be used. These may resemble, but may not be identical to, methods used in previous centuries because it is not only possible, but positively advantageous, to use modern ideas and technology in designing simple, cheap, portable machinery.

Types of sawmill

Major factors to consider in selecting a suitable sawmill
Only the cheapest small sawmills are considered here but, even with this size of mill, it is essential to take into account certain variables:

○ Size of log to be cut: small logs are relatively easy to move, easy to cut, require little power to cut, and can be cut with quite cheap equipment.
○ Hardness and heaviness of wood to be cut: the hardness of the wood determines, to a large extent, the rate at which it can be cut. Some tropical woods are very heavy, hard and difficult to cut.
○ Cost of equipment, reliability of operation and availability of spare parts: it is essential to get equipment that is reliable, durable, and that has either the back-up of a good spare-parts service or that can be repaired in local workshops.
○ Ease of operation and maintenance: the equipment must be operable and repairable by existing technicians possibly with some extra training. In particular the sharpening and tension-ing of saws is a skilled operation. The skills required are least for reciprocating saws, greater for circular saws and greatest for bandsaws. The smaller the circular and bandsaw blades are, the easier they tend to be to maintain, and the less maintenance they require.

Human and animal-powered sawmills
The pitsaw is the simplest human-powered sawmill. Other types have been made at different times although these have largely been replaced by mills powered by steam, internal combustion engines, water power or electricity.

Because pitsaws use human muscle-power inefficiently, some

[19]

consideration is currently being given to developing pedal-powered or 'rowing action'-powered mills which would be portable and more efficient than pitsaws. None are available yet, however.

The traditional pitsaw still in common use is a long (up to three metres/ten feet), usually tapered steel blade with a handle at each end (see Fig. 2.1 (b)). The saw is used vertically to cut along lines marked on a log by drawing a string rubbed in charcoal dust tight along the log and then pressing it onto the surface to give a black line. Logs are either tilted at one end (Fig. 2.2), rolled up a ramp, or supported on timbers over a pit which is dug underneath them (Fig. 2.3).

Pitsawing can be surprisingly fast and accurate if skilfully done and is still used in many parts of the world to produce large quantities of sawnwood. The only equipment required for pitsawing is a number of pitsaws, files to sharpen them, a tool for providing side-set on the teeth (which can be made very simply),

Fig. 2.2
Hand sawing a small log using a trestle.

[20]

axes and saws for felling trees, implements for digging the pits, and tools for rolling and turning logs.

Pitsaws are particularly appropriate where suitable trees are scattered, the country is mountainous or steeply sloping, roads are few or capital is scarce. In most developed areas of the world, however, pitsaws have been replaced by sawmills of one kind or other as these are more productive and take much of the hard work out of sawing. Sawmills can range in size from those costing hundreds of millions of US dollars to small mobile or portable mills costing only a few hundreds or thousands. In almost all parts of the world, the value of sawnwood is such that any reasonable production will repay a fairly high investment in machinery and equipment to produce it. The availability of suitable sawlogs is often the limiting factor in determining the

Fig. 2.3
A three-man pitsawing operation for large logs using a true pit

[21]

size of mill that should be used; the skills available to run and maintain machinery are vital in deciding what type of equipment can be operated profitably. Even the simplest equipment such as a pitsaw has to be imported into many developing countries, and the more complicated and expensive equipment becomes, the more difficult it is to operate and maintain and to obtain spare parts for. Any sawmill, therefore, should be as simple, robust and easy to operate as is consistent with producing the quantity and quality of timber required.

Water and wind-powered mills
These too were common in the past but are rare these days. Frequently used in the past was the mill powered by a slow-turning water wheel. Water turbines running at much higher speeds are now used in some places and can be used with direct drive to a sawmill, or to produce electricity to power the mill. The same can be true of windmills, but relatively large, costly structures are required to give enough power.

Steam-powered mills
These were common in the past but are rare these days. Heavy, costly boilers requiring constant attention and skilled supervision were used for the larger mills to which logs had to be brought rather than taking the mills to the logs. Traditionally the boiler furnaces were fed with saw dust or wastewood. No other fuel was necessary. Small portable steam engines are currently under development.

Mills powered by internal combustion engines
Diesel and petrol engines have now been developed which are light and easily transportable but which also generate a considerable amount of power. Chainsaw motors, mowing machine motors and small diesel engines can generate enough power to run circular saws and bandsaws and still remain fairly easily portable. They are, therefore, the most suitable forms of power for small mobile mills.

Producer gas power
Where petroleum fuels are very expensive or in short supply it is possible to run engines from producer gas made by passing a limited quantity of air over burning wood or charcoal. The larger

[22]

internal combustion engines will run quite well on producer gas, but costs of equipment tend to be high and the process not very efficient. Diesel engines burning gas have to use a mixture of about 30:70 diesel:gas, while petrol (spark ignition) engines can use 100% producer gas but lose some power in the process. New and improved gasifiers, which may be smaller and cost less than is currently the case, are in the process of being developed.

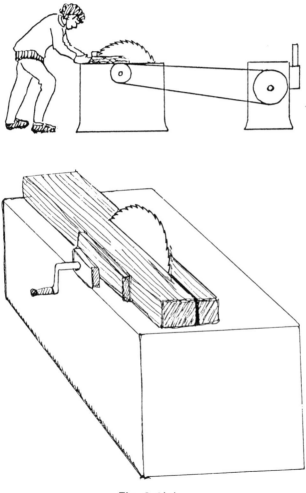

Fig. 2.4(a)
A simple circular saw bench

[23]

Choice of the right equipment

There is a wide choice of sawmill equipment available to suit different conditions but most of it is designed for sawmilling on an industrial scale and almost all requires some logging equipment to bring the logs to the saw; although mobile mills reduce the need for this, most are not so easily moved that they do not require some movement of the logs.

Mills for small logs

Where pitsawing is not very suitable, as for small logs, small circlar saw benches driven either by small diesel engines or by a vehicle power take-off are cheap and practicable. These consist of a saw, a saw spindle and two bearings bolted to a table through which the saw protrudes (Fig. 2.4 (a) and (b)). The spindle is driven by some means which could be by human or animal power, but is more usually motorized in some way. Simple saw benches, some of which are mounted on wheels and some of which are portable, can be bought from a variety of manufacturers.

'Rolling table saws' incorporate a table onto which the log can be clamped ('dogged') and which moves past the saw so ensuring a more accurate cut than is obtained by using a static table and 'fence' (movable rest against which the timber is pushed to give a measured thickness of cut equal to the distance between the fence and the saw blade). Rolling table saws can also handle heavier logs than a normal fixed-table saw bench. They are more expensive, however. Fig. 2.5 shows a rolling table circular saw bench.

Mills for large logs

Small logs can be moved relatively easily by human or animal power to the sawmill but large logs are heavy, often weighing several tons, and can be moved much less easily. A sawmill that can be moved to the log, therefore, is more attractive to the small operator. Increasing numbers of portable (i.e. lifted by hand or mechanically) or mobile mills (on wheels or trailers which can be towed) have been designed with varying degrees of portability and mobility. Few are designed to be moved to every log and most require some movement of logs to the saw as well. The pitsaw is completely portable, as are various chainsaw attachments designed for planking logs. A typical chainsaw mill of this type is shown in Fig. 2.6. Although the chain cuts out a wide

[24]

Adjustable distance piece

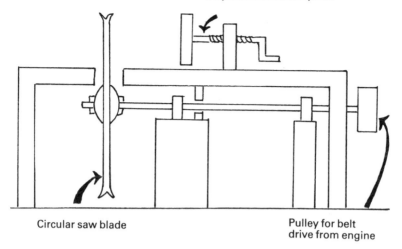

Circular saw blade

Pulley for belt
drive from engine

Fig. 2.4.(b)
Section through circular saw bench shown in 2.4(a)

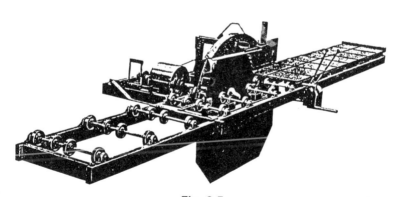

Fig. 2.5
A rolling table circular saw (E. Hole Ltd.)

[25]

Fig. 2.6
A chain saw used for ripping a log

Fig. 2.7
A recently developed portable bandsaw operated hydraulically
from a diesel engine on a wheelbarrow (ITDG).

[26]

The two saws are at right angles and start at the top of the log working across it and then move down to cut out a second layer from the log. The motor and saws run along a box girder beam over the log which is supported on solid steel beams at each end of the log which in turn are supported by four corner posts placed around the log. Raising and lowering of the beams allows vertical movement, and movement of the box girder beam along the steel beams gives lateral movement. Longitudinal movement is achieved by the motor and saw assembly running along the box girder beam.

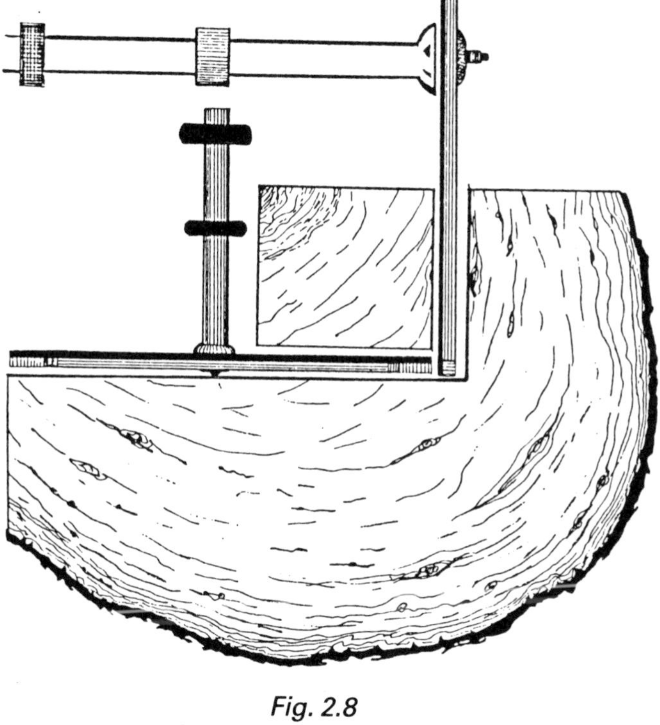

Fig. 2.8
A mobile double circular saw mill with two saws at right angles.

'kerf' (band of wood removed as sawdust) and leaves a rough surface on the timber, this type of mill is fairly cheap and is suitable for cutting timber of large dimensions which can then be split into smaller sizes by small machines or hand-sawing. It is therefore best used to convert logs to reasonably easily-handled sizes which can then be resawn to smaller dimensions by other methods.

Small bandsaws which are truly portable are now being made (Fig. 2.7). They are not more than two or three times the price of most chainsaw mills, and cut with much less waste, require less expenditure on fuel and produce a smoother surface to the timber than chainsaws. For some time portable sawmills, using two circular saws mounted at right angles to cut into the log from the top and work across the log in layers (see Fig. 2.8), have been used successfully. These mills are heavier and more costly than those described so far and require some logging equipment to feed them as well as motor transport to move them.

Many other types of mills are available, but these are more expensive and less portable and thus not considered to be within the scope of this book. At a simple level, there is a need for the design of improved hand- or animal-powered mills which would be more efficient than the pitsaw in using the muscle power available.

Methods of sawing

It is possible to saw up logs in different ways to give different grain patterns and different kinds of distortion on seasoning.

Fig. 2.9(a) shows different methods of cutting logs and the likely shrinkage on seasoning for the different cutting patterns after drying. Tensions in logs, knots and irregular grain will give further, less predictable distortion.

Normally logs are either cut through and through which gives a mixture of quarter sawn and flat sawn timber, or they are turned a few times to give faster cutting than true flat sawing or true quarter sawing. The 'industrial patterns' shown in Fig. 2.9(b) show two possibilities.

Flat sawing shows up annual rings or grain patterns as waves or irregular widely-spaced patterns, whereas quarter sawing results in a striped appearance from both annual rings and wider layers of 'interlocked' grain which alternately spiral left and right up the stem of the tree and reflect light differently. The mahoganies display this characteristic well.

[28]

Sequence of cuts   *After seasoning distortion*

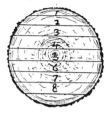   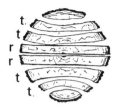

t — tangentially flat sawn cupping distortion
r — radially (quarter seam) little distortion

Turning for flat sawing — cutting method

Number shows sequence
of cuts. Distortion
similar to flat sawn
(tangential = t) wood
shown above.

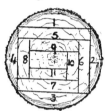

Quarter sawing cutting method

This method gives very
little distortion after
seasoning.

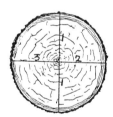

Fig. 2.9(a)
Methods of cutting and their effect on distortion on drying.
Through and through-cutting method

[29]

A quarter-sawn timber cutting pattern

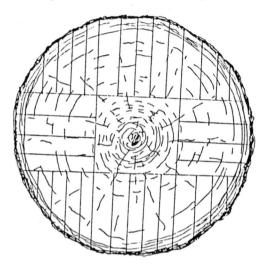

A flat-sawn timber cutting pattern

Fig. 2.9(b)
Industrial cutting patterns

Timber drying

Because wood shrinks as it dries (see Chapter 1) it needs to be dried to the moisture content at which it will remain during use, before it is made into furniture, joinery or any other article where stability is required.

Stacking

In order to dry timber it is first necessary to saw it into the size required and then stack it so that air can pass between the boards to evaporate water from the surface of the wood. This is done as shown in Fig. 2.10. The spacers placed between boards (known as 'stickers') should be lined up vertically so that the weight of the timber above is taken directly on a lower layer of stickers and does not bend the timber. They should be 20–25mm (1in) thick for normal timbers and should be 600–700mm (2–2.5ft) apart.

Air drying

Stacks of timber kept in open-sided sheds, or under waterproof stack covers which prevent rain falling directly onto the stack, dry by the passage of air at normal outside temperature and humidity over the timber. As the rate of drying depends on the climate, obviously hot, dry climates will allow faster drying than cold, wet ones. The moisture content which the timber eventually reaches, below which it will not go in a particular climate, is known as the 'equilibrium moisture content' (emc). In most moderately humid tropical countries where trees grow this is 16–20%mc. In the same countries the emc of wood inside a closed building is about 12%mc.

Kiln drying

It is therefore necessary, if complete drying to 12%mc is to be obtained, either to bring the wood into a closed building for several months after first air drying to 20–25%mc, or to dry the wood to 12%mc in some kind of 'seasoning kiln'. This takes the form of a chamber where the temperature is raised and the humidity lowered to speed up drying and to make it possible to dry to 12%mc. Heating can be by steam, hot water, exhaust gases, solar heat, electricity or electricity combined with dehumidification (condensation of the water in the kiln air by cooling and then reheating the dry air with the heat removed

[31]

Side view of stack

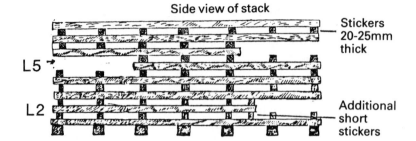

Stickers
20-25mm
thick

L5

L2

Additional
short
stickers

Plan view at L5

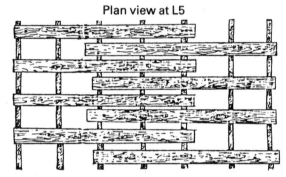

Procedure

1. Build base of stack on firm land surface with stack bearers running across the stack and at least 100-150 mm (4 – 6 inches) square in section. Free air flow under stack is essential.

2. Length of stack should be the length of the longest piece of timber to be dried.

3. Stickers should run across the stack between boards in vertical rows   600-750mm (2 – 2.5 feet) apart.

4. Shorter timber should alternately be pulled to each end of the stack as shown in plan view of L5 above to retain square-ended stack with all board ends supported.

5. Overhanging board ends should be supported by additional short stickers where there is danger of drooping of the ends (L2).

6. Stacks should be covered with some waterproof cover to keep off direct rainfall.

Fig. 2.10

Method of 'box stacking' different lengths of timber for drying.

[32]

from the water by condensation during the cooling process. The water is then drained away as liquid.)

Although most kiln drying entails expensive equipment and high running costs, solar kiln drying is possible, particularly in the tropics, at a fairly low cost. The principle of a simple 'greenhouse'-type solar dryer is shown in Fig. 2.11. This can be made up quite easily but does require electricity to drive the fans necessary for air circulation. Wind is too unreliable as a method of driving fans and although solar-generated electricity is suitable it is too expensive at present. Once wood has been dried, it is essential to store it under the conditions of temperature and humidity in which it will be used. Wood at over 20% moisture content is much less resistant to rot and insect attack than at lower moisture content.

Wood preservation and finishes

Many woods are not used, or only partly used, because they rot or are easily attacked by insects. This explains why such a small proportion of the many species of tropical woods are currently used. Most easily-rotted woods are easy to treat with preservatives. For furniture the protection required is less than that for building timber or timber that is to be exposed to the elements.

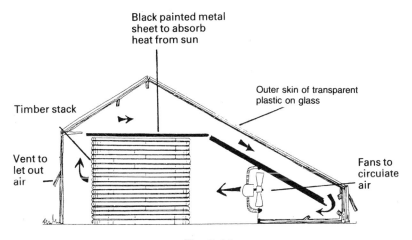

Fig. 2.11
Simple solar-heated timber drying kiln (Oxford Forestry Institute).

[33]

The chief hazards to wood in the tropics are:

○ rot if in contact with water, damp floors or walls;
○ log-boring insects which attack logs before they are cut up into timber (only attack green, wet logs);
○ sapwood borers (attack green or dry sapwood);
○ termites (attack green or dry sapwood or heartwood).

To protect furniture a colourless, clear wood preservative is needed. Some locally made oils may be suitable or Borax, a simple, harmless chemical used for medical purposes, can be dissolved in water and painted onto the wood after which it can be polished, varnished, painted or oiled. The solution used should be about 5 parts by weight of Borax dissolved in 100 parts by weight of water. Linseed oil is commonly used for treating woods. Even ordinary diesel oil is a good preservative provided the smell is acceptable. For most furniture, a brush coat of preservative is adequate but it may be that the main points of hazard such as the bottoms of table and chair legs, bookcase bases, and cupboard backs require more thorough treatment by soaking in a preservative. Much depends on how well-protected a house is and where the furniture is placed. Protection from damp and a termite-proof floor reduce the hazards to furniture very considerably, but even with this protection sapwood borers and dry wood (non-ground living) termites are a hazard. It is very important therefore to ensure that wood is properly prepared and used. Seasoning and protection from rot and insect attack are especially crucial to a good quality and durable product.

CHAPTER THREE

The workshop and its equipment

It is axiomatic that the work a man produces is only as good as the man himself. Therefore it must be emphasized that without conditions conducive to good work, a man is unlikely to use even the best tools to best advantage. It makes good sense then to apply modern methods and proven principles of ergonomics (the study of man in relation to his work environment) along with good, reliable traditional tools.

The workshop

Of primary importance is the provision of appropriate workshop conditions with shelter from the sun, rain and wind yet with adequate ventilation, heating or cooling, and lighting. Clearly, the design and construction of the workshop will vary with local conditions, but in every case, a firm, level floor is obviously a great advantage. A continuous effort should be made to keep the workshop as clean and tidy as possible, not only for health and safety reasons but because a tidy workshop, with proper provision for storage of tools and materials, will improve not just the appearance of the workshop but the quality of the work produced. As this too will be directly affected by the physical well-being of the workers, it is also worthwhile to provide workers with rest, washing and toilet facilities (the VIP or ventilated improved pit, as devised originally for Zimbabwe but now widely used in Africa, meets the latter need admirably). Once these basic requirements are satisfactorily met, it is then time to plan and equip the workshop.

Hand tools

Man has been a tool-making animal for over two million years and during that time has evolved a variety of simple but effective tools, many of which are still in widespread use. These include saws, knives, chisels, hammers, planes, files and various forms of axes.

The tendency in industrialized countries has been to evolve mechanically-powered versions of these traditional tools in order to increase output and decrease the input of human effort and skill. The disadvantages of this practice in developing countries are becoming increasingly evident: the insecurity of dependence on finite sources of energy, increasing unemployment and difficulties in maintaining sophisticated equipment.

Hence, for those countries struggling to improve their standard of living without massive input from outside, the best course of action is reliance on traditional hand tools and on human muscle power and skills. There is scope for improvement in output, in ease of operation and in maintenance by the right choice of tools and their use. The following section describes basic hand tools and is followed by a section on complementary equipment, designed to improve the efficiency and use of these tools.

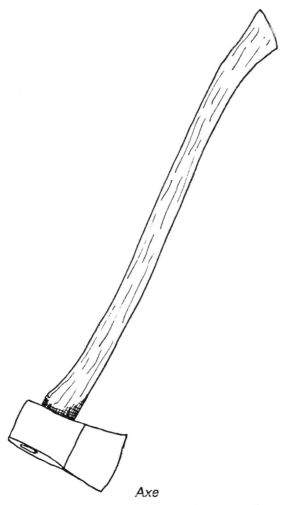

Axe

The shape and size of the axe head varies according to its use,
e.g. for felling trees; for splitting wood; or for shaping and
smoothing wood such as barrel staves and wheel spokes.

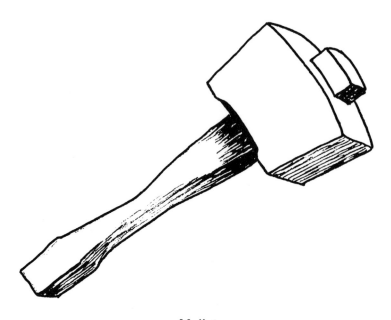

Mallet
Used to drive chisels and to drive pieces of wood into other pieces of wood.
The wood carver's mallet has a rounded head.

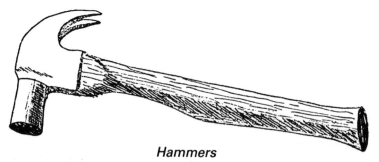

Hammers
The claw hammer is the everyday hammer for the carpenter.

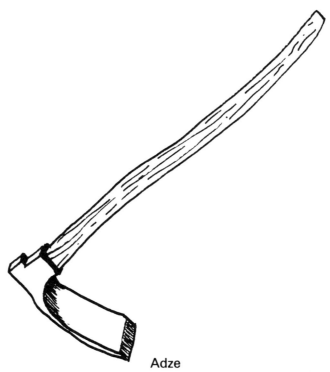

Adze

Used for smoothing and shaping planks of wood.
In skilled hands it is a versatile and accurate tool.

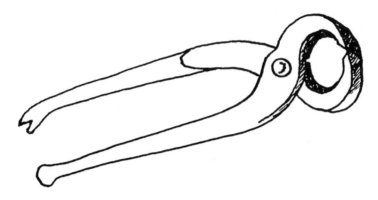

Pincers
Designed primarily to remove nails from wood.

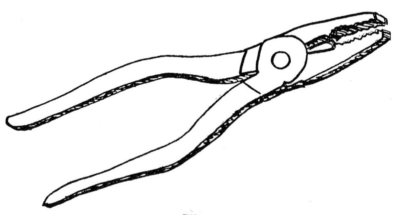

Pliers
Designed to grip and bend metal and to cut wire.

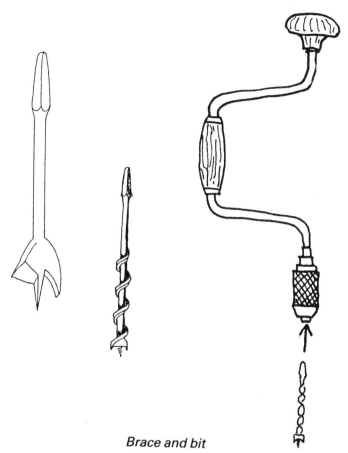

Brace and bit

For boring holes from 0.5cm up to about 5cm in diameter.
Maximum depth of hole about 15cm.

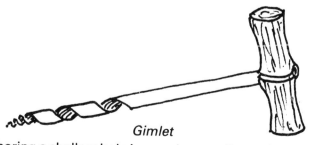

Gimlet

For boring a shallow hole in wood – usually to take a screw.

[41]

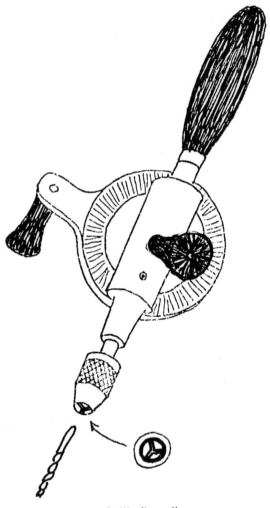

Drills (hand)

For drilling small diameter holes up to 1cm diameter. The drill
commonly used for drilling holes for screws.

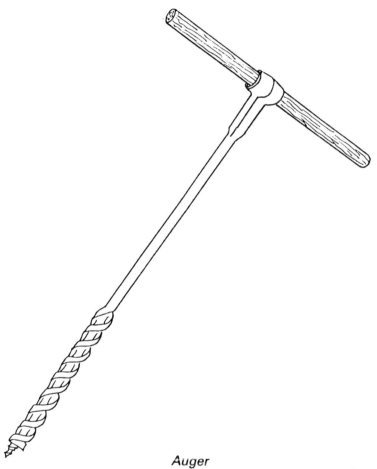

Auger
For drilling holes in wood. Diameters from 1.25cm to 6.5cm.
Shaft about 60cm long.

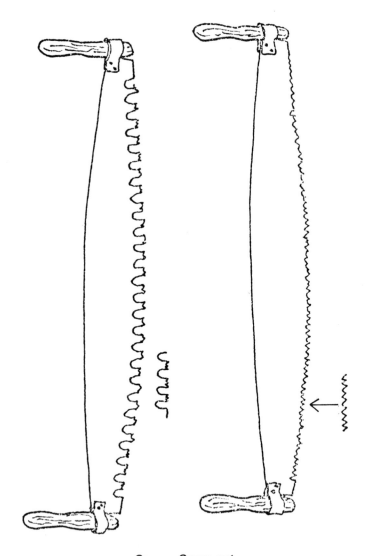

Saw – Cross cut

For cross-cutting. Blade of saw about 1 to 1.5 metres long.

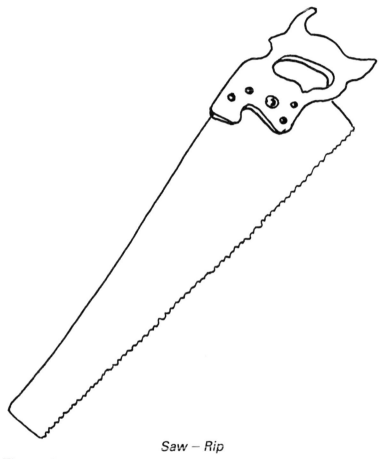

Saw – Rip

The teeth are set to make it easy to use when cutting along (i.e
in the direction of) the grain. Length 50 to 70cm.

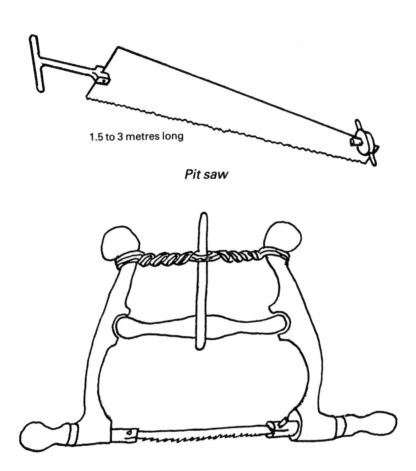

1.5 to 3 metres long

Pit saw

Bow saw

The carpenters bow saw is used for cutting wood into shapes.
Not to be confused with the forester's cross-cut bow saw for
felling trees and cross-cutting them into lengths.

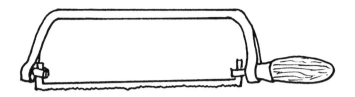

Hacksaw

A metal-working tool. Can be used on wood, but cuts very slowly. Not to be confused with the bow saw. Frames are of different sizes (from 15 to 50cm) to take blades of different lengths.

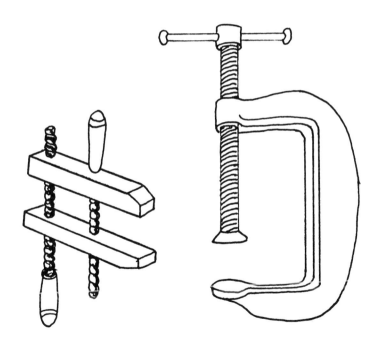

Clamps

For holding pieces of wood together. Particularly useful in holding joints together whilst glue is setting (drying).

Saw – Keyhole

For cutting holes in wood e.g. keyholes. Blade about 30cm long.

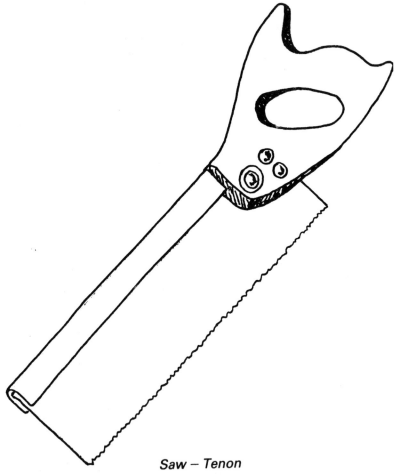

Saw – Tenon

A fine-toothed saw for fine work and cutting small-sized pieces of wood. Length 25 to 40cm.

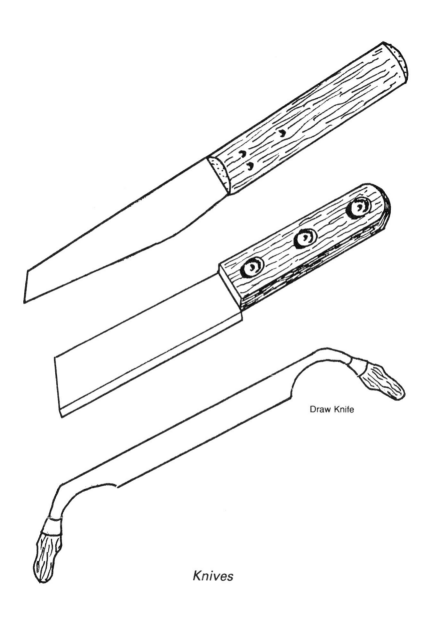

Draw Knife

Knives

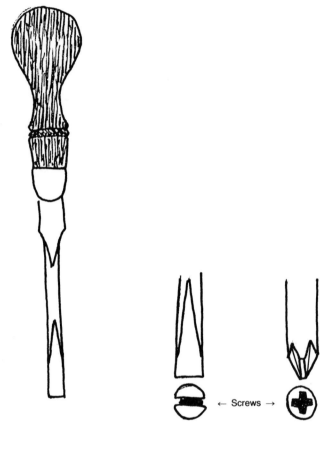

← Screws →

Screwdrivers

Two types; the ordinary blade and the cruciform blade (Philips screwdriver). Length varies from less than 15cm to over 50cm.

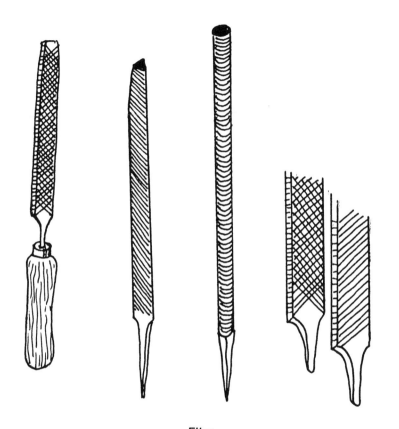

Files
For sharpening saws the two basic files are the flat file and
the *triangular file.*
For filing wood, rougher files (or rasps) are used. They may be
flat, round, half-round or triangular.

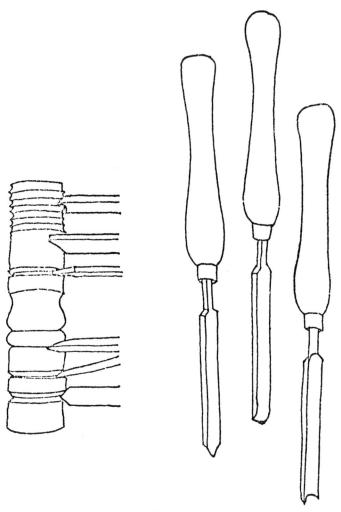

Chisels
A basic tool for shaping and cutting e.g., mortises and tenons.
Comes in many shapes and sizes. Used in wood turning.

Rules
For measuring.

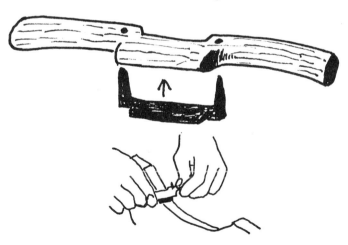

Spokeshave
For shaping wood (see also Chapter 2).

[53]

Block plane

For cutting end grain. Length 9 to 20cm. Cutting iron width 2.5 to 4cm.

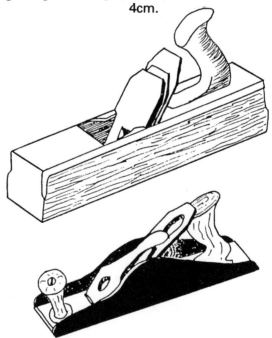

Jack plane

To dimension wood i.e. to shave it to an exact thickness and width. Length 36 to 45cm. Width of cutting iron 5cm.

Rasp

For shaping and smoothing wood. May be of solid metal or
have a renewable blade attached by screws to a handle.

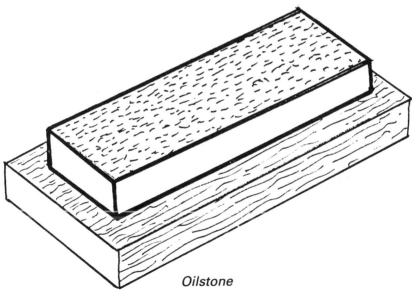

Oilstone

For sharpening most edged tools but especially knives and
chisels.

[55]

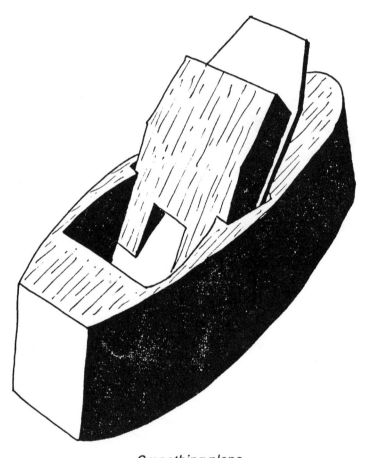

Smoothing plane

To plane timber to a smooth surface finish. Length about 25.5cm. Cutting iron width 4cm to 6cm.

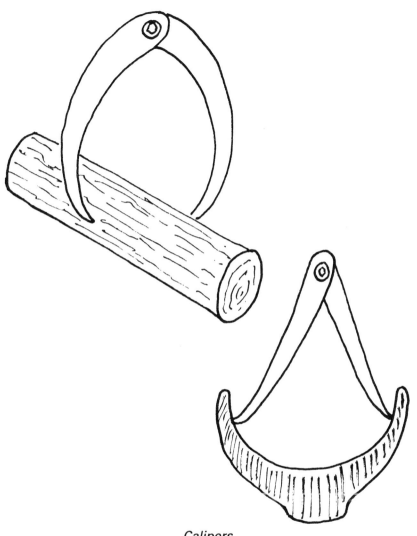

Calipers
For measuring diameter or thickness.

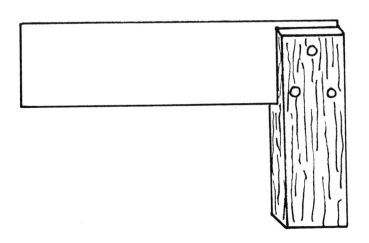

Set Square
For marking and measuring right angles.

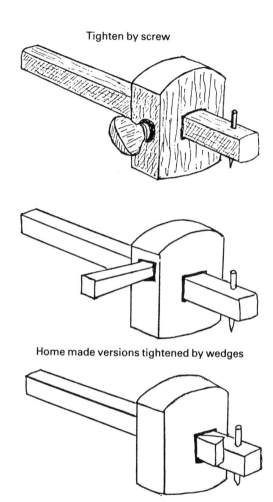

Tighten by screw

Home made versions tightened by wedges

Marking gauge
To mark wood where wood is to be cut.

Complementary equipment

As any workman knows, the anvil is more important than the hammer. In the same way, it is true that nearly all hand tools require for their optimum use some form of complementary equipment, usually designed to support the workpiece in the best possible way for ease of working, e.g., a bench and vice. The importance of such holding devices must not be underestimated. Among the advantages is higher productivity resulting from the use of a tool to its best advantage. A firm support for sawing, filing, or hammering will ensure that less energy is dissipated in movement of the support or in vibration, and this energy will appear as useful output. Equally, there will be a clear physical advantage to the operator in having the workpiece at the best height to avoid his having to stoop or stretch, and to allow his use of the right muscles in their best mode.

The general principle to remember when supporting a workpiece is the need for both *mass* and *stiffness*; for example, a chopping block needs to be as heavy as possible but itself also needs firm support. Sometimes a tree stump with roots still embedded, cut level to the correct height depending on the length of timber to be split, may serve usefully for this. Another good alternative is shown in Fig. 3.1, where a section of a tree with a triple fork is cut to size so that, when inverted, the three branch stumps provide firm tripod support however uneven the ground.

For sawing felled timber to length, some form of sawing horse is desirable; this might take the form of the simple design shown in Fig. 3.2 where three sets of crossed members provide V-notch support for timber of long or short lengths. The diagonal bracing provides rigidity against side sway.

Other effective forms of clamping devices for cleaving with a froe or shaping with a draw knife are described in the section on cleaving, but this technique is only applicable to straight-grained timber. With other timbers sawing and planing are the chief methods employed and for these a suitable workbench and clamping device are desirable. Fig. 3.3 shows a basic design of bench; note that it achieves mass and rigidity by the use of thick sections for the legs and top, and is further stiffened by an apron plank fastened to the front edge of the bench top and to the front legs. It is essential to have the bench top at the right level, about 90cm for workers of an average height of 175cm, but higher or

[60]

lower for others—generally at about one half the worker's height.

With the bench, a variety of holding devices may be usefully employed. The simplest is a bench stop, a square-section peg carefully fitted to a square hole in the bench top. The peg can be tapped upwards to provide a stop for the workpiece being planed or tapped below bench level when not in use. Another simple device is a bench hook, Fig. 3.4(a), which is placed on the bench top when sawing small pieces of wood with, for example, a tenon saw. A metal bar bent to the shape of a question mark (?) and fitted to a hole in the bench top, Fig. 3.4(b), makes a simple form of clamp. When the hooked part is placed over the workpiece and the clamp is tapped downwards, the vertical stem jams in the hole and clamps the workpiece firmly; yet it can be released easily by tapping the clamp from below.

When something more than these simple devices is required, a vice (or vise) is the common method for holding the workpiece

Fig. 3.1
Simple workpiece (e.g. chopping block) provided by inverted section of tree with triple fork.

[61]

firmly (Fig. 3.4(c)). This is true especially with a chisel where, for safety reasons, it is necessary to keep both hands on the tool. Obviously it is necessary for the workpiece to be firmly clamped.

Most vices use a large screw thread on a main shaft, turned by a capstan at the outer end. Because with this they require precision-made sliding members to provide parallel motion of the jaws, all modern vices are factory-made in steel and are quite expensive to produce and transport.

Earlier European designs of vice were made entirely of wood, including both the main shaft of large diameter with screw thread and the sliding members. It may be possible to copy these designs locally, by using suitable hardwood and machining the screw threads onto the shaft and mating the members in a workshop equipped with a screw-cutting lathe.

A still earlier form of vice avoided the use of slides altogether by using long vertical members, hinged together at their base near ground level and carrying the jaws at their top end.

Fig. 3.2
Sawing horse

[62]

Although the jaws remain parallel in plan view, they are not strictly parallel in end view but this will not matter as long as the fixed jaw has a plane face and the other is slightly curved—the workpiece should still be held firmly.

A possible alternative to the use of screw threads is a pair of wedges with the same wedge angle. When opposed and tapped at opposite ends a large clamping force can be applied with parallel motion of the outer surfaces. Such pairs of wedges, known as folding wedges, have been widely used in the past for clamping purposes, e.g., for a sash clamp, and would be quite effective as a modern screw clamp. Two other simple vices, both tested in prototype, are shown in Figs. 3.5(a) and (b) and 3.6(a) (b) and (c).

Bench vice using bicycle and chain
Fig. 3.5(a) and (b) show a simple design of vice based on the use of a bicycle rear wheel, sprocket and chain to exert a large clamp

Note square peg bench stop (a), bench hook (b) and clamp (c).

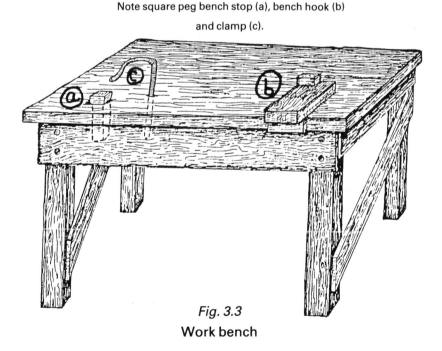

Fig. 3.3
Work bench

[63]

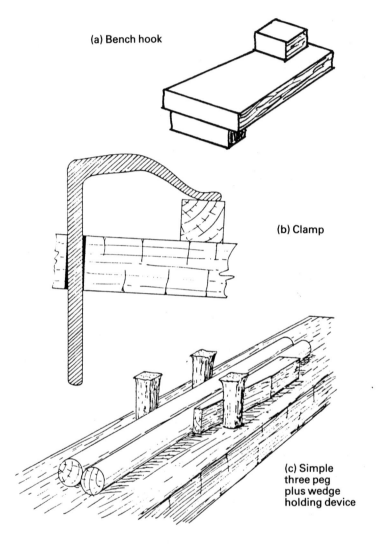

(a) Bench hook

(b) Clamp

(c) Simple three peg plus wedge holding device

Fig. 3.4

force at the jaws. The jaws are constrained to give a near-parallel motion by being mounted on pairs of long vertical members connected at ground level by a block of wood and a metal plate which acts as a hinge.

The rear triangular part of a standard bicycle frame is mounted below the bench top as shown, with the rear wheel (complete with sprocket, freewheel and tyre) mounted in the reverse of the customary way (i.e., chain on left side, as seen from above). Two further freewheels, with their pawls removed

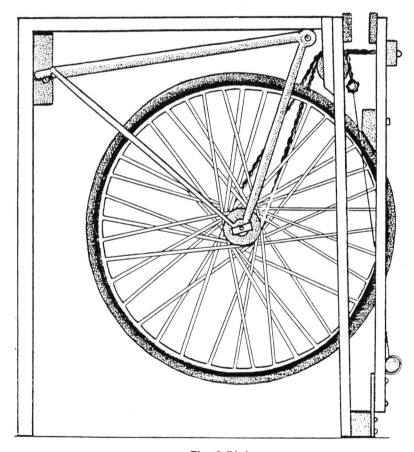

Fig. 3.5(a)
Bench vice side view

[65]

to allow free movement in either direction, are mounted side-by-side on a wooden bar of circular section which is in turn clamped to the front apron plank of the bench top. The plank is slotted to accommodate the sprockets with the lower end of the slot bridged by a metal strip to restore strength in bending.

One end of a bicycle chain is fastened to the centre of a strong yokepiece bridging the two outer vertical members. It is then led over one free sprocket, round the sprocket on the wheel, back

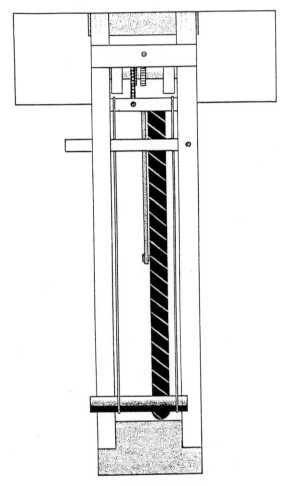

Fig. 3.5(b)
Bench vice Front View

[66]

over the other free sprocket and then anchored to a steel pipe acting as a yoke between two cords. The latter lead down to a wooden bar or steel pipe near ground level, which acts as a footbar. A wedge is hinged at one end to one of the vertical members and protrudes beyond the other vertical members. This wedge will jam the tyre to prevent rotation, but can be released by raising one end.

In use, the workpiece is placed between the jaws and is first clamped by pressing down the footbar, thus taking up the slack in the chain by rotating the freewheel sprocket on the wheel. Then final tightening is achieved by pulling up on the protruding section of the wheel and tyre; the jamming wedge prevents the wheel running back. A leverage ratio of over 8:1 results from the relative diameter of sprocket and rim; hence a large clamping force should be obtainable. This design appears to offer a very simple low-cost bench vice.

Bench vice using twisted cord or catgut
The drawings (Fig. 3.6(a) (b) and (c)) show a prototype made at Oxford University Department of Forestry to a design by Stuart Wilson. The principle used to exert a large clamping force is similar to that of the so-called 'Spanish windlass' traditionally used to tension the blade of a frame saw—twisted cord or catgut using a short stick or fid at the centre of the twisted double cord.

In this bench vice, the jaws are at the upper end of two long planks joined at their lower ends by a sheet metal member which forms a hinge. (The prototype uses a channel section, but a better design is that shown in the drawing of the alternative design of bench vice, Fig. 3.5(a), based on use of a bicycle wheel and chain; this uses a flat metal plate fastened to a rigid wooden block).

Below the outer jaw is a wooden capstan with tommy bar. The inner end of the capstan is slotted and pinned to carry a loop of strong cord (e.g., fishing line) or catgut Fig. 3.6(b). The other ends of the cord are led over pulleys on short arms under the bench top and then through holes in the back plate and out to anchorages on the face of the front plate. Effective anchorages are formed by short nails with large flat heads (felt nails). By this means the force at the jaws is effectively doubled, so a large clamping force can be exerted by turning the capstan to twist the cord or catgut. Friction keeps the capstan from turning back-

[67]

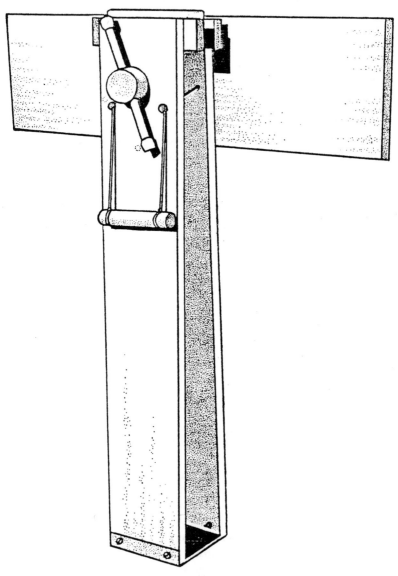

Fig. 3.6(a)
Bench Vice

wards; to release the workpiece, the capstan is turned backwards to unwind the cord.

A problem arose of retaining the cord in the grooves of the pulleys; a solution was the use of nails close to the pulley rim and of a fifth nail on the centre line to prevent the cords from twisting asymmetrically. This modification is shown in Fig. 3.6(c). A neater design would incorporate wider and longer supports for the pulleys, to allow room for the nails close to the pulleys and with a single bridge piece to locate the centre nail.

Once a workpiece is shaped to size, most constructions require joining whether by gluing, nailing, screwing, pegging or by a shaped joint such as dovetailing or mortice-and-tenon. During

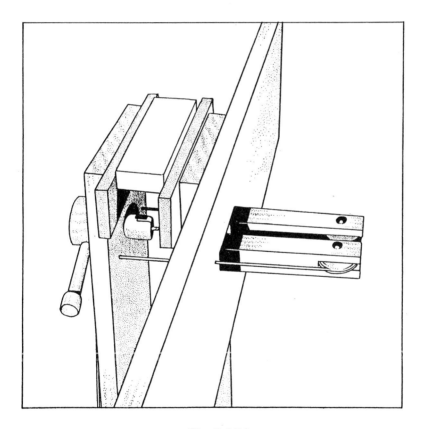

Fig. 3.6(b)

[69]

assembly, particularly when glue is to be used, some form of clamp will be needed at each joint. A sash clamp (so called because it was originally used for sash windows, but which is of much wider utility, e.g., for clamping together planks to form a table top) has already been mentioned. Another very useful common clamp is the G-clamp, so called because of its form. Factory-made clamps use a cast steel frame and steel screw and are therefore expensive. A simple alternative is the 'F' clamp shown in Fig. 3.7, where an L-shaped member is made from

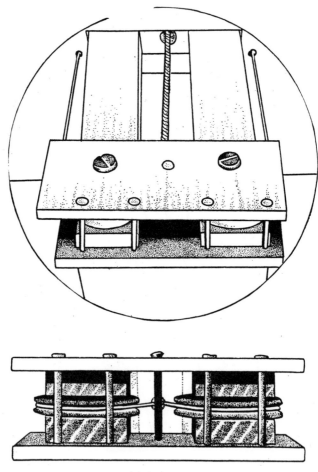

Fig. 3.6(c)

[70]

suitable planed timber and carries a sliding member to form the lower jaw. The sides of the mortice in this sliding member are slightly curved on opposing narrow sides in such a way that downward pressure on the jaw causes jamming. Thus a clamping force can be exerted by tapping the lower jaw upwards, while the pressure can be released by tapping downwards on the projecting heel of the sliding member.

Methods of making many of these tools and complementary devices are described in detail in two ITDG publications by Aaron Moore *How to make twelve woodworking tools* and *How to make planes, clamps and vices* (Intermediate Technology Publications, London, 1986, 1987).

It is not, of course, necessary for every workshop to have all the tools and equipment described in this chapter; much can be accomplished with only a few of the simplest tools. A start can be

Fig. 3.7

F Clamp

[71]

made with just the minimum and much of the complementary equipment can then be constructed and expanded as the workshop grows in size and manpower. Most craftsmen like to have their own kit of favourite tools, but some of the less-used items can be shared.

Having described the workshop and its equipment the next chapter describes some of the common processes of wood-working, i.e., how to make use of these tools and equipment.

CHAPTER FOUR

Woodworking methods

Woodworking can be divided into three classes of work: *carpentry* includes the building of structures such as buildings, bridges, platforms, etc.; *joinery* includes house fittings such as doors and windows, which demand finer work than carpentry, and also simple furniture making; *cabinet making* is the skilled joinery needed to make good quality furniture. There are also specialist woodworkers such as wheelwrights (who also make carts and wheelbarrows), shipwrights (large craft), boatbuilders (small craft), coopers (who make barrels, tubs, etc.), hurdle makers, fence makers (including gates), broom makers and picture framers.

Each trade employs its own techniques although many of the tools and their uses are common. Although nowadays most timber for woodworking ('lumber') in industrialized countries is supplied in lengths sawn to a particular cross-sectional size and shape, formerly this was not the case. Logs were trimmed by an axe or adze to the size and shape required, or were sawn to the thickness of plank needed by using a pitsaw, as already described.

Cleaving and sawing—tools and equipment

Traditionally, much rural woodworking has been accomplished by the technique of cleaving (splitting or riving) instead of sawing. Such methods, adapted to the resources and needs of the locality, are already widely used in developing countries. However, various tools and equipment have been developed in the UK that may not be widely familiar but which could help to improve productivity if adopted.

Potential advantages of cleaving

The potential advantages of cleaving are:

Simplicity of tools The tools needed for cleaving are essentially simple—wedges (including a wedge with a handle, or froe), and a mallet or beetle. For further shaping, a selection of draw knives or spokeshaves, planes and chisels are used; all these are simpler

[73]

to make and sharpen than any form of saw.

Durability Splitting the wood along the grain is not only much faster than sawing but does not weaken the wood, either structurally or through exposure to the weather; hence cleft-wood structures last much longer than sawn work.

Uses
Hurdles, fences, gates, stiles, cribs.
Rakes, hay forks, brooms, crooks, walking sticks, tool handles.
Ladders, wheel spokes, tent pegs, clothes pegs.
Cooperage: barrels, tubs, pitchers, etc.
Buildings: posts, beams, roof members, shingles (wooden roof tiles).
Carts, sledges, coracles, trugs.

Suitable timbers
Crucial to the success of cleaving is the availability of sufficiently straight-grained timber, relatively free from knots. The lack of such timber may well be the main limitation of this technique in some areas.

For many purposes timber of small diameter is preferred, so trees which are naturally small, saplings, thinnings or coppiced woods are used. The technique of coppicing, i.e., regular cutting, leaving each stump to grow a new crop of several straight, upright branches, is a very old custom which is being revived because of the high productivity of the permanent root structure.

Larger sections, e.g., oak and beech, can be split by suitable wedges and then further reduced by means of a froe (Fig. 4.1), an effective tool which deserves wider recognition. The initial split in the round log is started by means of a number of small steel wedges (using a steel hammer), then a large wooden wedge is used to widen the split (using a wooden mallet). When the log has been reduced to smaller sections, the froe is hammered into the end grain and then the handle is used as a lever to twist the narrow wedge-shaped blade in the split in order to open it up.

Returning to the more usual methods of woodworking, sawn timber is used for most carpentry work, but for joinery it is usually necessary to smooth the surface of the wood and reduce it to an exact size by use of a plane. When the timber is supplied ready-planed by a planing machine, care should be taken as the

[74]

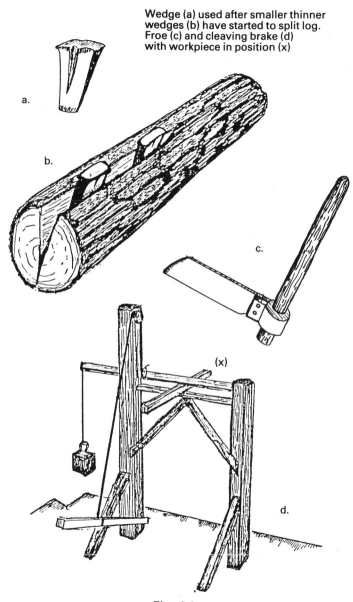

Wedge (a) used after smaller thinner wedges (b) have started to split log. Froe (c) and cleaving brake (d) with workpiece in position (x)

a.

b.

c.

(x)

d.

Fig. 4.1

actual dimensions may not be exactly the same as those given. Thus it is essential to measure each piece before using it.

Cutting to length is normally done with a cross-cut saw; finer cutting, such as for a tenon, an overlapping joint or a mitred joint (as used at the corners of a picture frame), is done with a tenon saw. For this purpose the workpiece is held either by means of a bench hook or in a bench vice.

All fine work is done on a bench, using an appropriate method of holding the workpiece firmly; this is especially important when using a chisel or gouge (a chisel of curved section). All edge tools need to be kept sharp by means of an oil stone. Occasionally they may require grinding on a grindstone; this is a skilled operation and should be attempted only by a qualified craftsman. This applies also to the sharpening of twist drill bits.

Wood turning

The use of a lathe to produce wooden articles of round section is very ancient, widespread and extremely versatile. Among useful items that can be made quickly and cheaply are the following:

Industrial goods Wheel hubs, pulleys, spindles, bobbins, rollers, dowels, tool and brush handles, etc.

Domestic goods Chair legs and spars, stools, knobs, towel holders, lamp bases, bowls, plates, mortars and pestles, salt and pepper pots, napkin rings, bangles, wheeled toys, spinning tops, etc.

The earliest type of lathe is probably the fiddle bow lathe (Fig. 4.2). Another simple, traditional type is the pole lathe (Fig. 4.3), the main feature of which is the use of a springy pole which supports the upper end of a rope or leather strap. The rope is wrapped around the workpiece, which is supported between centres, with its lower end fixed to a treadle that is itself hinged to the ground. The operator presses the treadle with his foot, thereby rotating the workpiece towards him and enabling a cut to be made by a chisel supported on a tool rest. At the end of the stroke when the operator raises his foot, the springy pole returns both the treadle and workpiece to their starting positions ready for the next stroke.

The drawing shows a simple, basic design in which the lathe bed consists of two stout timbers supported by splayed legs at either end (or by vertical posts buried in the ground). The headstock and tailstock consist of short, vertical posts with their lower ends shaped to fit the lathe bed and retained in position by

[76]

wedges inserted into slots below the lathe bed. The headstock carries a stationary steel shaft with a conical end which engages with a conical hole at the centre of one end of the workpiece; a similar steel centre is carried by the tailstock, but this is adjustable by means of a screw thread, so as to allow mounting, adjustment and release of the workpiece.

Before mounting, the workpiece is first shaped roughly with a drawknife to a circular section to reduce tool chatter (vibration) and to allow a smoother drive by the rope or leather strap. The toolrest takes the form of a wooden bar fixed between headstock and tailstock; alternatively it may consist of a third movable block clamped to the lathe bed and carrying a T-shaped member, adjustable in height. The chisels have long wooden handles to give the operator a firm grip; the outer end of the handle is tucked under the arm and held against the body. Although the basic form of chisel has a rounded end, others may have straight or pointed ends depending on how the workpiece is to be shaped.

For bowls or similar shapes of larger diameter, a flanged drive shaft is held firmly against the workpiece, which is held in place by a number of spikes, in order to form an assembly which can

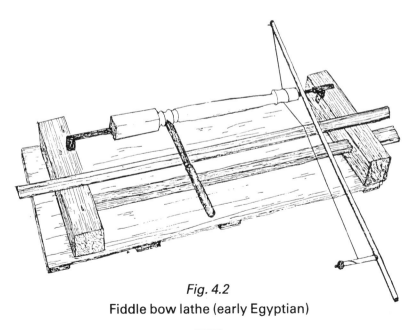

Fig. 4.2
Fiddle bow lathe (early Egyptian)

[77]

Fig. 4.3
Traditional pole lathes

provide the necessary rotation speed, and access for the tool to the workpiece.

The main drawback of a pole lathe is that cutting takes place only on the downstroke of the treadle. Therefore a treadle lathe in which the workpiece always turns in the same direction is a distinct improvement; a continuous movement can be achieved either by means of a crank and flywheel or by a ratchet mechanism. The latter is used in a design given in an ITDG handbook (*How to make a wood-turning lathe* by Rob Hitchings, Intermediate Technology Publications, London, 1986). This lathe is largely in welded steel and its construction should be within the capability of most small workshops with basic steel fabrication equipment and skills.

An alternative version can be made largely from wood on the lines of the traditional pole lathe, but using bicycle parts in a similar way to that shown in the ITDG handbook.

Crank-drive treadle lathe
This is a design for a wood-turning lathe which can be made simply and cheaply in a developing country, using readily-available materials and simple techniques of manufacture. Wood is the main material and standard bicycle components are the main source of precision components. As shown in Figs. 4.4(a) (b) (c) and (d), the basis of the design is the use of the rear part of a standard bicycle, retaining both pedals, chainwheels and rear wheel. This assembly is mounted upside down under and to the rear of the lathe bed in such a way that the left pedal can be connected to the treadle and the rear wheel rim acts as a pulley to the lathe spindle by means of a belt. The right crank carries an added weight (not shown in Fig. 4.4) to balance part of the weight of the connecting rod and treadle. The rear wheel uses a fixed sprocket rather than one with a freewheel in order to utilize its flywheel effect. In order to increase this effect, extra weight can be added near the rim by using two steel hoops made from 10mm diameter rod or similar materials, fitted just inside the rim and held in place by lacing wire through the spokes.

If greater power is needed, and an assistant is available, the right crank can be used as a handle to provide extra input. If such extra power is needed frequently, the right crank could be connected to a further treadle assembly by means of another connecting rod, thus increasing the power through improved ergonomics.

[79]

Construction is almost entirely from square-section timber, e.g., 50 × 50mm, preferably of hardwood, planed; about 18m length is needed. The joints would preferably be bolted but, if not, glued and nailed. A second alternative would be the use of trenails (wooden pegs) slotted at each end with a wedge driven in to tighten them in the holes, as with hammer-heads, stool legs etc. (Fig. 5.4).

As the treadle assembly has to withstand considerable twisting, it is advisable that the corner joints be mitred and reinforced by gusset plates above and below, either of metal fixed with screws or of plywood glued and nailed; the T-joint would be butted and reinforced with gusset plates above and below. The lower end of the connecting rod is clamped to a standard left

Fig. 4.4(a)
General view of crank driven treadle lathe

[80]

pedal carried on its crankpin and crank. The latter is fixed firmly to the treadle arm by means of a bolt fitted through the crankshaft hole (⅝in diameter, about 16mm) using a tubular sleeve if necessary to get a good fit. The other end of the crank is fastened by means of a U-bolt or pipe clamp, leaving enough of the crank projecting to allow free movement of the pedal and connecting rod. The latter is conveniently formed of two wooden strips fastened onto either side of the upper and lower pedals.

The bicycle frame is cut through just forward of the saddle clamp and the bottom bracket. It is fastened to the lathe bed supports by means of steel angle brackets fixed to the uprights, having slotted holes by which the rear axle is clamped, allowing

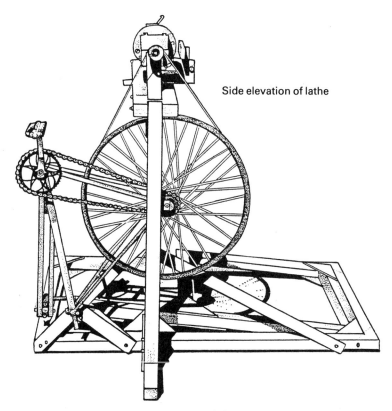

Side elevation of lathe

Fig. 4.4(b)
Treadle lathe

[81]

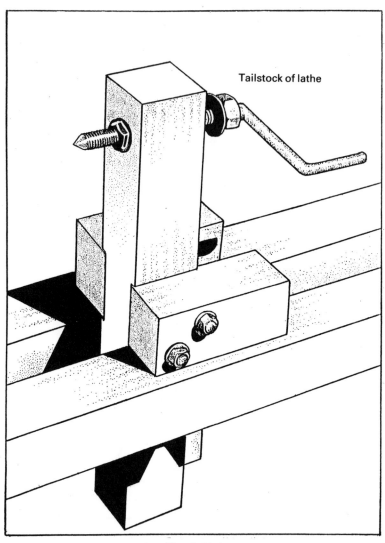

Fig. 4.4(c)
Treadle lathe

adjustment for the belt tension. The lower apex of the bicycle frame is fixed between the two sloping members using a long bolt through the saddle clamp, with tubular spacers.

Lathe bed
This is formed of two parallel members, 50mm apart. The movable tailstock and toolrest may be clamped into position by means of a wooden wedge under the bed, working through a slot in the tongue which projects through the gap between the bed members. The tongue of the toolrest is thinner to allow adjustment for different workpiece diameters and also to allow slewing of the toolrest when turning a piece mounted on the face plate. Alternatively a bolted toolrest assembly may be used.

Headstock
The main problem here is the choice of bearings; previous designs have used bicycle bearings, either a complete bottom

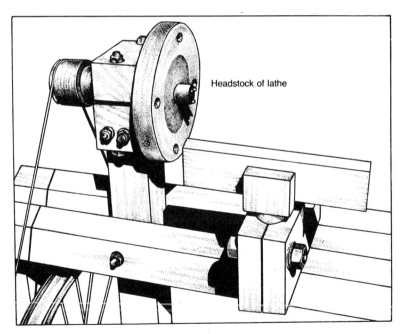

Headstock of lathe

Fig. 4.4(d)
Treadle Lathe

[83]

bracket with shaft (which means destroying a bicycle frame for just this purpose) or a front-wheel hub and axle. In either case the outer housing can be clamped onto the headstock pillar with the driving pulley and chuck or faceplate fixed at opposite ends of the shaft. The advantages of using such bearings are ease and cheapness (unless it means sacrificing a good bicycle frame!), as well as ease of adjustment and replacement. On the other hand, they are not precision-ground bearings and are not designed for high speed use (the bottom bracket would normally rotate at about 60 r.p.m. and the front wheel at about 150 r.p.m.). Consequently they may have limited life, and may be noisy.

Alternatives include the use of a pair of standard ball bearings (e.g., as used in car dynamos) fitted to a steel shaft, as shown in the figure. Such a unit would have to be made in a workshop equipped with a metal-working lathe, but is otherwise a simple process. Ready-made units may be obtainable in certain cities since they are made for mounting grindstones.

The drawing shows the first prototype, made by Dr. Andrew Dunstan, at the cost of about $30 for components and 42 hours of labour; testing is underway but the design seems sufficiently promising to be included here.

Complementary equipment
As important as the tools themselves are suitable devices for holding the workpiece in a convenient and ergonomic manner, to enable the operator to maximize production and minimize effort. The most obvious requisite is a chopping block.

If a workpiece is too long to use on a chopping block, a cleaving brake may be used to hold it horizontally (See Fig. 4.1(d)). A horizontally-pivoted lever is weighted at one end to clamp the workpiece against a fixed platform; the weighted arm can be raised to release the workpiece by means of another lever.

Further shaping is accomplished by some form of shaving with other tools such as an adze, a side axe, draw knife, spokeshave, plane or chisel (Chapter 3). Traditionally the adze was widely used for shaping curved items such as chair seats and ship timbers as well as posts, beams and roof trusses for buildings.

With a draw knife, an upright brake Fig. 4.5(a) or, more commonly, a shaving horse (Fig. 4.5(b) and Fig 4.6) are widely used. The shaving horse consists of a low trestle and a pivoted

[84]

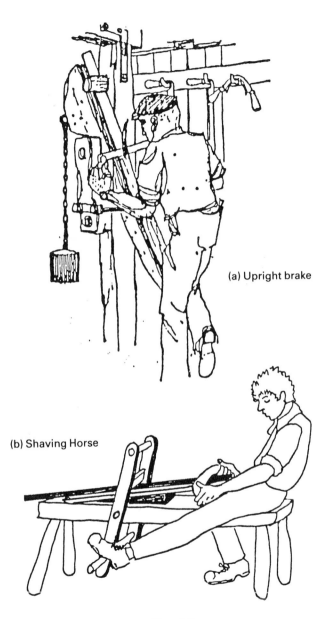

(a) Upright brake

(b) Shaving Horse

Fig. 4.5
Holding devices

[85]

Fig. 4.6
Shaving horse (detail)

lever carrying, at its lower end, a foot bar, and at its upper a block forming the upper jaw of a clamp; the lower jaw is fixed to the body of the horse. In use, the operator sits astride and presses, usually with one foot, on the foot bar, thus clamping the workpiece between the jaws. When he pulls on the knife his foot presses hard and thus increases the clamping force; yet the workpiece is easily freed by simply removing his foot. Some versions use a lump of wood to act as a counterbalance in order to control the backswing. The clamp-release-clamp operation is quicker than a screw-operated vice and leaves both hands free.

For shaving very long strips, the nearly vertical form of brake is sometimes preferred (Fig. 4.5(a)) where the clamping lever is operated by the knee and a weight is used to open the jaws when required.

Other versions of the shaving horse have two horizontal members to raise the workpiece to a convenient height. As well as for shaving, other versions are used for various clamping purposes, e.g. for binding besom brooms.

Another means of shaping tool handles to a smooth circular section is by using a stail engine, a form of rotary plane (Fig. 4.7(a) (b)). The finished diameter can be varied by means of the screwed handles clamping the two halves of the plane body; a tapered handle can be produced.

For small-diameter dowels or rake tines, a simple but effective device is a tine shredder (Fig. 4.7(c)). These dowels serve well as trenails for joining timber members; the ends of the dowels may be split and forced apart by a thin wedge for using to fix chair legs to the seat, or hammer heads to the shaft.

Another simply-made tool of the greatest utility is described by W.J. Wooldridge in his book *Woodturning*. He terms it the 'spearpoint general-purpose tool'; as shown in Fig. 4.8, it consists of a narrow point, about 1.5mm (1/16in) wide, hollow-ground at the end of a flat tongue about 25mm (1in) long. It may be made from a worn file of square section, about 250mm (10in) long.

Among its uses are parting-off finished work, for roughing down blanks, for fine turning of spindle work and for quickly hollowing out bowls and other objects mounted on the faceplate. In this last use, successive cuts are made with the tool perpendicular to the faceplate and at 45° to it; so that rings of triangular section are successively removed from the centre outwards. This

[87]

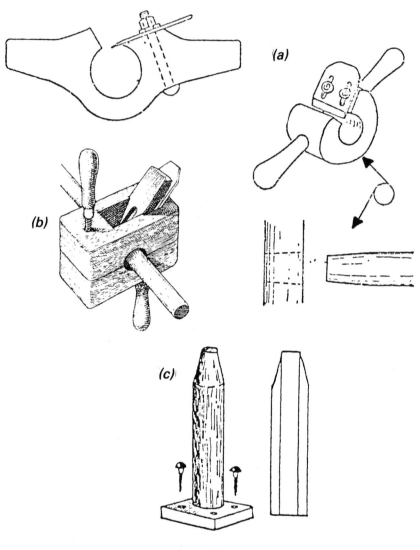

Fig. 4.7
Stail engine for making round handles or for tapering
round handles (a) and (b) Tine shredder (c).

saves time and effort in removing material such as shavings.

Finish

For many potential users the finish of a piece of woodwork is important for the acceptance of the product and in promoting careful use and maintenance. For goods that are to be sold, particularly for export, a high standard of finish is essential.

For outside use, the natural surface of timber poles, with or without the bark, may be acceptable and functional; this method is sometimes valued in developed countries as 'rustic work'. Its life depends on the species of timber and on the climate, but this may be extended by treatment with a preservative, as described in Chapter 2.

For external woodwork of a building, such as window frames and doors, where the timber has been planed and thus the grain ends exposed, a more definite method of preservation is called for. Traditionally such woodwork is painted but this requires proper initial and subsequent treatment, i.e., sanding to a smooth surface, and the application of a primer, undercoat and topcoat, reapplied every few years, depending on the climate and the exposure. A recent development is the impregnation and staining of timber, a process which is claimed to reduce maintenance very greatly, but the necessary preservatives and stains may not be readily available.

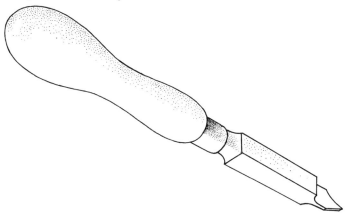

Fig. 4.8
Spearpoint general-purpose tool

[89]

For indoor furniture, a smooth finish is usually desirable and also some form of surface treatment—painting, varnishing or polishing. Modern polyurethane varnishes or lacquers, if available, are easy to apply and give very durable polished surfaces that are resistant to wear, moisture and decay.

Some products may with advantage be stained before polishing, particularly if the natural colour of the wood is very light. In some areas, natural dyes may be available for this purpose. For other items of furniture, bright paintwork may be attractive according to the local traditions and tastes. The variety of possibilities is immense—contrasting areas, geometrical patterns, floral themes, graining, etc. The only limitation is the skill and imagination of the painter. For repetitive patterns, stencils may be used. Toys especially benefit from the imaginative use of bright colours, but care must be taken that the paint contains no lead. Whatever finish is chosen, careful application will ensure good and saleable products.

CHAPTER FIVE
Furniture

Every country has its own styles of traditional furniture which reflect the kinds of materials readily available and the particular skills of local craftsmen. For example, where cattle are numerous, beds and chairs are often made of leather stretched over wooden frames (Fig. 5.1(a) and (b)). The purpose of this chapter is not to attempt to catalogue and describe the many types of local furniture and other everyday items made of wood. Rather it is to describe briefly some basic ideas and techniques for making simple items out of wood—such as beds, chairs, stools, benches, tables—which come high on the list of man's requirements after his needs for food and shelter have been satisfied.

Where basic needs have to be met by hand-made furniture, it is obviously wise to avoid designs that have been evolved primarily to take advantage of highly-mechanized methods shaping and joining wood, or to show off the skill of the craftsman in producing intricate shapes. It is also desirable to avoid where possible designs that rely on imported or hard-to-come-by fastenings (e.g., screws) or metal components, such as brackets or framing. Some common types of joint are shown in Fig. 5.2 and nails and screws in Fig. 5.3.

The simple examples shown here are all old and well-tried but they represent only a few of the many locally-developed designs that have successfully met local needs over long periods of time. Some of the simple, classic designs—like the three-legged stool— are of course also in production in highly mechanized workshops and still find a ready market in industrialized countries.

In Chapter 4 methods of cleaving wood are described. Cleft wood can be used in place of sawn wood for most of the items described in this chapter. The round wood that is the basis of many of the designs may be obtained by rounding sawn or cleft pieces of wood with a draw knife. Alternatively the wood may be turned on a wood-turning lathe as described in Chapter 4. The use of round turned pieces of wood of for example 2 to 5cm in diameter to make parts for stools, benches, chairs and tables has

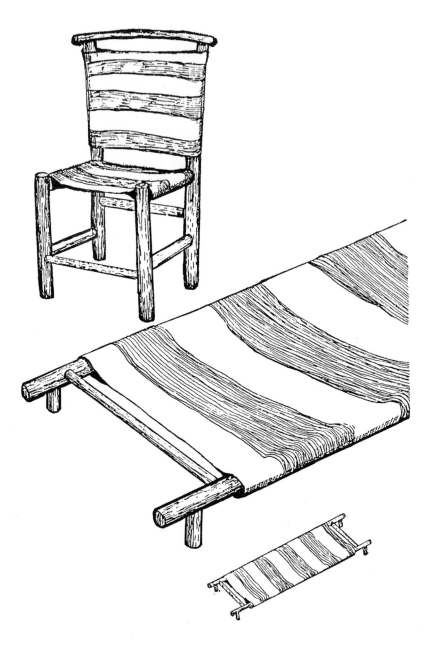

Fig. 5.1(a)

several advantages, e.g., strong structures can be built up from quite small pieces, using only the simplest of tools.

The joints are kept tight by wedges, glue, shrinkage or a combination of these techniques. Thus the legs of the three-legged stools may be held in place by wedges as may the horizontal bracing pieces in four-legged pieces of furniture (Figs. 5.4 and 5.5). When the shrinkage method is used the pieces of wood in which the hole is drilled are not completely seasoned

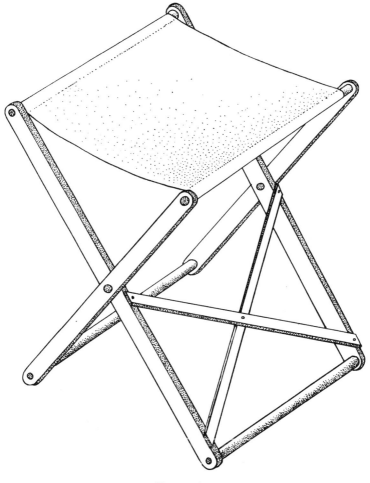

Fig. 5.1(b)

[93]

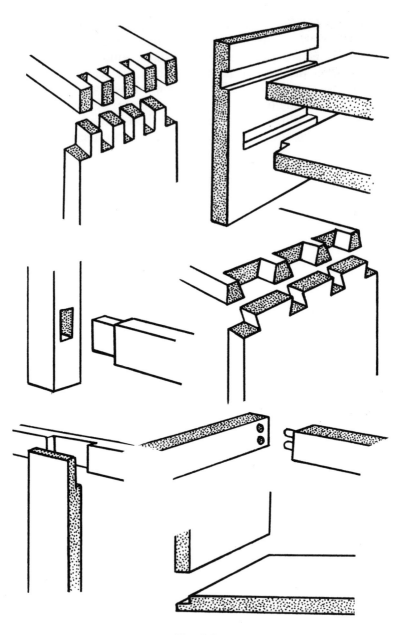

Fig. 5.2
Some common wood joints

whereas the pieces of wood which fit into the holes are thoroughly dried. The joint is made as tight as possible at the time of assembly. As the not-quite seasoned wood dries out, it shrinks and grips the other piece of wood very tightly. The relative degree of dryness between the two pieces of wood is a matter of local experience, trial and judgement, for if the difference in dryness between the two pieces is too great the forces generated during drying may cause splitting, and the joint then becomes loose.

The use of wooden pegs or dowels driven into pre-bored holes produces strong lasting joints. Pegs or dowels are not, as is sometimes thought, inferior to nails, screws or other metal fasteners (Fig. 5.6(a)).

Trying to avoid the use of any kind of joint at all can bring penalties in that usually much more wood is needed to perform a given function. Where wood is plentiful, however, very simple robust items such as benches and tables can be made with a minimum of tools (Fig. 5.6(b)).

Wood that is not completely dry when it is assembled will in time shrink as it dries out. If wedges have been used to tighten the joints these may be driven further in or replaced with slightly

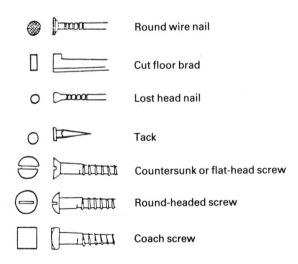

Fig. 5.3
Common types of nails and screws

[95]

Fig. 5.4

[96]

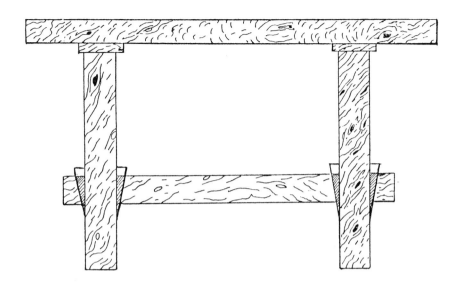

Fig. 5.5

[97]

thicker wedges. If square sawn timber is used the vertical
members have a rectangular slot cut in them just big enough to
receive a horizontal piece of wood (Fig. 5.5) which is itself
provided with four rectangular slots. The position of the slots is
such that when the longitudinal brace is inserted in the slots in
the legs it can be held by wedges driven into the four slots.

Alternatively the slots may be made vertically.

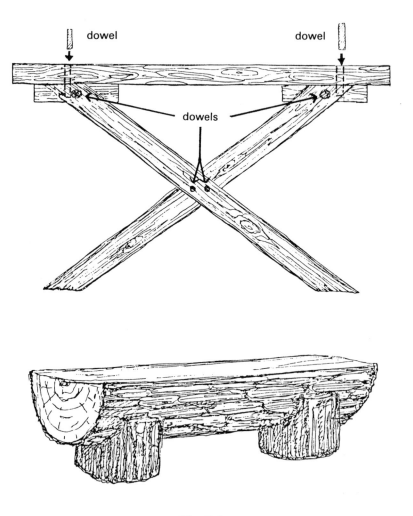

Fig. 5.6

[98]

Meat- or food-safe

Much food is wasted through poor storage methods, particularly in tropical countries but also during hot weather in temperate countries. Among the devices evolved to reduce deterioration, a fly-proof safe can be very effective in the absence of refrigeration or other proven methods such as drying, salting, smoking, bottling or canning. In addition, it may be arranged to keep food as cool as possible by siting it in shade, exposed to any wind which may blow. A further degree of cooling can be achieved by evaporation (see below).

The accompanying sketch (Fig. 5.7) shows a possible design made of wood. It consists of a skeleton framework which is covered with panels of fly-screen material which must be both rot- and rust-proof, e.g. plastic mesh or stainless steel gauze. The hinged door must also be fly-proof, i.e. the catch must be secure, the door must fit closely to its frame and any gap should be filled by using a padded strip.

The safe is roofed over with two sloped panels of wood, metal or plastic, or with locally available thatching of grass or leaves, to keep off sun and rain. These roof panels, which should extend at least 10cm beyond the walls on all sides, are supported by triangular panels above the door and back panel of the safe. A ridge member gives a strong, sealed joint between the roof panels and also provides strong points for two screw eyes or staples for hanging the safe, and for a central hook inside for hanging the meat or food.

The floor of the safe is slatted and lined underneath with a fly-proof panel. A slatted shelf may also be provided at half-height if the food is not to be hung from the central hook.

In order to reduce attack by ants or other insects, the whole safe may be slung from a bracket or branch of a tree. Alternatively, the safe may stand on a platform supported by an upright pole with a band of grease around it to prevent attack by insects.

For evaporative cooling a rectangular piece of cloth or other porous material is wrapped around three sides of the safe (not the door). The lower edge dips into a water tank under the floor of the safe, placed between the legs but extending beyond it to make the water level visible and to allow ease in filling.

This is a good example of a very simple but effective device that can be adapted to individual circumstances and materials.

[99]

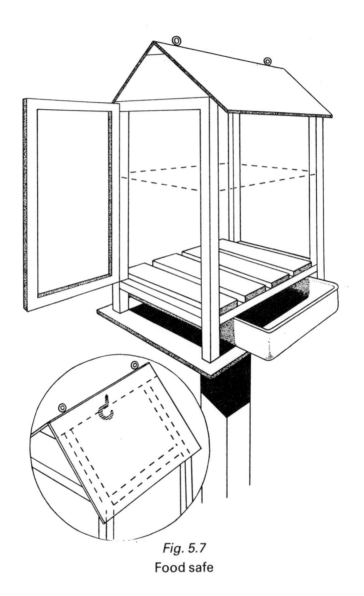

Fig. 5.7
Food safe

Jointing

Although simplicity of design and of manufacture characterizes the furniture described, the articles are in no way inferior to more complicated factory-produced furniture. Certainly in the rugged conditions of the village they will perform as well as, or better than, many of the items made for urban houses. They are also generally suitable for use in schools, hospitals and other institutions where wear and tear is usually heavier than in domestic environments.

Until the middle of this century, furniture parts were still being made by individual craftsmen working in the woodlands near to their source of raw material in a number of industrialized countries; these were generally round components turned on pole lathes (described in Chapter 4) and were sold to furniture factories in nearby towns. Brush handles and brush heads were similarly made in or near the woodlands for sale to factories which made them up into the finished article for the consumer. Combining rural craft fabrication of simple components with mechanized factory production of the final article can give the craftsman cash-earning opportunities that he would find difficult to match if he had to make and market the whole article himself.

It is hoped that the simple designs of basic furniture illustrated or described in this chapter will give some idea of the sort of items that can be made using the tools and equipment described in earlier chapters. It is not intended that designs be copied exactly; they should be modified in light of local experience. There is a vast range of everyday things that can be made from wood with hand tools and lathes and other equipment powered by human effort. Even if there is no access to timber cut in a sawmill, techniques such as pit-sawing or cleaving can reduce the round log to shapes and sizes of timber that can be worked on the carpenter's bench or in simple lathes.

The capital value of the tools and equipment is small compared to that needed to equip the most modest of mechanized woodworking shops. Yet provided that the wood is then adequately seasoned the quality and the durability of hand-made articles is as good as and sometimes superior to those made by machine.

[101]

Annex

Conversion Table 1 (Inches to millimetres)

Conversion factor: 1in = 25.4mm

inches	mm	inches	mm	inches	mm
1/16	1.5	0.10	2.54	1	25
1/8	3	0.20	5.08	2	50
3/16	5	0.30	7.62	3	76
1/4	6	0.40	10.16	4	101
5/16	8			5	127
3/8	10	0.50	12.70	6	152
7/16	11	0.60	15.24	7	177
1/2	13	0.70	17.78	8	203
9/16	14	0.80	20.32	9	228
5/8	16	0.90	22.86	10	254
11/16	17			11	279
3/4	19	1.00	25.40	12	304
13/16	21			18	457
7/8	22			24	609
15/16	24			36	914

Conversion Table 2 (Millimetres to inches)

Conversion factor: 1mm = 0.0394in

mm	inches	mm	inches
1	0.04	100	3.94
2	0.08	200	7.87
3	0.12	300	11.81
4	0.16	400	15.75
5	0.20	500	19.69
6	0.24	600	23.62
7	0.28	700	27.56
8	0.31	800	31.50
9	0.35	900	35.43
10	0.39	1000	39.37
20	0.79		
30	1.18		
40	1.57		
50	1.97		
60	2.36		
70	2.76		
80	3.15		
90	3.54		
100	3.94		

Conversion Table 3 (Metres to feet and feet to metres)

Metres	feet	feet	inches	Metres
1	3.28	1	0	0.30
1.1	3.6	1	1	0.33
1.2	3.9	1	2	0.36
1.3	4.3	1	3	0.38
1.4	4.6	1	4	0.41
1.5	4.9	1	5	0.43
1.6	5.2	1	6	0.46
1.7	5.6	1	7	0.48
1.8	5.9	1	8	0.51
1.9	6.2	1	9	0.53
2.0	6.6	1	10	0.56
		1	11	0.58
3	9.8	2	0	0.61
4	13.1	3	0	0.91
5	16.4	4	0	1.22
		5	0	1.52